THE LATIN-CENTERED CURRICULUM

A Home Schooler's Guide
to the
Classical Curriculum

Andrew A. Campbell

Non Nobis Press
www.LatinCentered.com

ISBN #: 1-930953-71-2

To my daughter, Julia, and my goddaughter, Annabelle

Ut ver dat florem, studium sic reddit honorem.

5

ACKNOWLEDGEMENTS

Et mihi dulces ignoscent, si quid peccaro stultus, amici. —**Horace***

In many ways, this book is not my own. It is a response to the needs of a community of parent-educators, and they deserve much credit for whatever is good and useful in it. I wish to offer my thanks to the members of the LatinClassicalEd mailing list for their support, enthusiasm, and helpful feedback on an early draft of this book. Stephanie Medcalf encouraged me in the crucial early phases of writing. Elizabeth McKeeman challenged me to defend Latin-centered education against the claims of multiculturalism. Sarah Schira sent helpful pointers on poetry and reminded me to stay playful. I especially thank the individuals who gave permission for me to quote their posts and those who shared their families' schedules.

Thanks are also due to my church family, who held me up in prayer during the writing and publication of this book. Ali Langsather shared her expertise in Latin pedagogy. Romy Holzer listened patiently as I ranted about the foibles of modern education. Melanie Krumrey's unfailing encouragement and hospitality more than once lifted me out of the writerly slough of Despond.

I also thank Ian Philips for sharing his memories of studying Euclid at St. John's and for teaching me to appreciate that very Roman genre, satire.

Two special teachers deserve mention here. Claude Fredericks first introduced me to classical Greek more than twenty years ago in a freshman poetry class at Bennington College, and Katherine Roberts led me on the upland march through Greek grammar, as far as Ithaka. Both have my undying gratitude; without their tutelage at key moments in my life, I most certainly would not have written this book.

Last, but not least, my deepest appreciation goes to my wife, Anne, for her faith in me as a writer and for trusting me with the education of our daughter. *Si vales, valeo, anima mea.*

---

* "I hope my dear friends will forgive me if I should make some silly mistake."

CONTENTS

Latin Centered Curriculum
Visit www.LatinCentered.com for direct links to resources mentioned in this book. Learn from other Latin-Centered families and contact the author through our forums and blog.

PREFACE

As a child, I did not have the benefit of the kind of education I describe here. In fact, with very few exceptions—the odd European colleague, tutor, or college professor who, despite having reached a venerable age, refused to retire—I know no one who did. In writing this book, I feel rather like the witch of Endor, calling forth the shade of some dead prophet, in hope that his wisdom will enlighten the current educational Dark Age.

Despite my own lack of formative classical education, I did manage, by hook or by crook, to get a little Latin and a little more Greek. A whirlwind summer intensive in graduate school, a delightful group tutorial fueled by strong coffee, online study groups for home schoolers and their parents, leisure hours in the company of Loeb editions and Penguin Classics paperbacks: These have been my Academy, my Lyceum.

I assume that my readers are, like me, the recipients of a "good enough" education, whether public or private. Our educations have been good enough to see us through to adulthood and into parenthood. They have been good enough to allow us to pay our way to apartments or houses, cars, computers, and, perhaps, student loans. And they have been good enough to awaken in us the evergreen parental hope that our children will have something better, something we didn't have but will sacrifice much to win for them.

So I want to encourage you. Even if you did not imbibe classical learning with your mother's milk—and let's be honest, few of us did—you can still give your child a solid grounding in the subjects and disciplines that make for a true education. You can move beyond vocational training and edutainment. You can trust that whatever you are able to do to move toward that shimmering El Dorado, the "ideal classical curriculum," will be a step in the right direction.

Start from where you are. If you are just investigating home schooling for the first time, I urge you to read widely and to take the time to think over what sort of education you want for your child. What is your vision of an educated person? What methods have a proven track record of producing such persons?

If you are moving from a neoclassical curriculum to a Latin-centered one, rest assured that you don't have to do everything at once. You do not have to jettison subjects that your students enjoy; if you have an elementary-age student who lives for science, then, bless you, give her science. If you are nervous about letting go of your grammar curriculum or spelling program, don't. Give Latin its due—the best hour of your students' day—and then judge for yourself what is necessary for *your* students in *your* home school.

My other piece of advice is to consider self-education as part of your student's education. Despite the proliferation of excellent self-teaching curriculum packages, classical education presupposes the presence and active involvement of a committed teacher. You will be teaching by example, by deed as much as by word. Let your student see you at the breakfast table, poring over your own Latin grammar books with your spouse. Let him hear you reading high-quality literature aloud to the family after dinner. Let him observe you grappling with big ideas as you discuss books together. Let her see your devotion to her, to her education, and to the Good, the True, and the Beautiful. Let her hear you pouring your heart out in prayer for knowledge and wisdom. Let her see what inspires you. Whatever the method, such dedication lies at the heart of all education worthy of the name.

A.A.C.
June 6, 2005

Boldface titles.
The first mention of a book or program package is given in boldface, to help readers who are scanning the text for book titles identify the "must-buy" resources for each grade.

I. PROLEGOMENA: TOWARD A DEFINITION OF CLASSICAL EDUCATION

Ἀρχὴ ἥμισυ παντός. —**Hesiod***

❧

What exactly is "classical education"? If you ask home educators, they might mention the Trivium and possibly the Great Books. They will talk about a rigorous, college-preparatory curriculum with a strong emphasis on critical-thinking skills and written expression. If they are classical home schoolers themselves, they will probably have read popular guides like *The Well-Trained Mind* or the essay that sparked the neo-classical revival, Dorothy Sayers' "The Lost Tools of Learning."[1] Many, however, will be unaware that Sayers' ideas represent a radical redefinition of the term "classical education." This new definition is so different from the one known to anyone born before this century, that it would have perplexed most of the writers who now populate our Great Books reading lists—and indeed, many of Sayers' own peers. Since classical educators profess to be looking to the past for inspiration and guidance, this chapter will provide a very brief overview of the history of classical education with an eye to defining the term in light of that history.

Greco-Roman Foundations: Education as Enculturation

The roots of classical education, like those of so many enduring arts, are to be found in ancient Greece. For the Greeks, *paideia* meant far more than what we usually mean by "education" in English. Rather than

---

* "The beginning is half of everything", or as the saying goes, "Well-begun is half-done."
1. The full text of Sayers' essay can be found at http://www.gbt.org/text/sayers.html and has also been reprinted in the appendices of Harvey & Laurie Bluedorn, *Teaching the Trivium: Christian Homeschooling in a Classical Style* (Muscatine, IA: Trivium Pursuit, 2001) and Douglas Wilson, *Recovering the Lost Tools of Learning* (Moscow, ID: Canon Press, 1991).

simply conveying a body of knowledge or a set of skills, the *paideia* of the ancient Greeks offered membership in a culture. Its goal was to bring children (and in most cases, that meant citizen boys) into the fold of the *polis*, the independent city-state, as virtuous and able citizens. "*Paideia*," writes classical education apologist Tracy Lee Simmons, "was about instilling core values, enunciating standards, and setting moral precepts."[2]

> The Greeks and Romans made sure to teach their offspring not only practical skills for getting along; they made them memorize poetry commemorating the deeds of their mythological and historical heroes. They filled their children's minds with "useless" information, by rote, with one purpose among others: to make them members of a people, to make them one. We cannot view classical education aright unless we factor in this element of culture.[3]

The Greek formulated the goals of this educative process not just in political terms, but also in spiritual ones: "[T]he supreme goal of education was happiness, which was conceived of as health of soul, the ultimate good man can hope to attain during his lifetime."[4] Plato defined education as a process by which the student is "rightly trained in respect of pleasures and pains, so as to hate what ought to be hated, right from the beginning to the very end, and to love what ought to be loved."[5]

The Greek terms for general education, *enkuklios paideia* or *enkuklios mathemata*, were later taken over into Latin as *liberales artes* and from there into English as the liberal arts.[6] These seven arts—grammar, rhetoric, dialectic, arithmetic, music, geometry, and astronomy—were already established as the general educational program from the fourth

---

2. Tracy Lee Simmons, *Climbing Parnassus: A New Apologia for Greek and Latin* (Wilmington, DE: ISI Books, 2002), p. 40.

3. Simmons, p. 37.

4. Simmons, p. 54.

5. Quoted in Simmons, p. 56.

6. H. I. Marrou, *A History of Education in Antiquity* (New York: Sheed & Ward, 1956), p. 244.

century B.C.[7] They were preceded by a course of primary education (*grammatistike*, learning to read and write, as opposed to *grammatike*, grammar proper[8]) and might be followed by higher rhetorical or philosophical studies, or by a period of physical training and military service, as in the Athenian *ephebia*.[9]

The Romans adopted much of the Greek educational model for their own. Just as *paideia* does not mean quite the same things as our "education," neither does *educatio* cover the same semantic field. It "referred not to schooling and intellectual progress but to the physical rearing of the child and his or her training in behaviour."[10]

Greek, the *lingua franca* of the Eastern Mediterranean, was as important in Roman schools as Latin, with some educators suggesting that children begin their studies with Greek, since they would acquire Latin naturally in the course of daily life. Wealthy Romans might engage a Greek nurse or tutor for their young children.

> The well-organized educational system of the [Roman] Empire had for its main aim to teach the two literary languages and to inculcate in the minds of all its pupils the established methods and desirability of imitation.[11]

The *doctrina duplex* or double course of study dictated that an educated person must know both Latin and Greek, and this was to remain the norm for two millennia—that is, until only a few generations ago.[12]

How was this program of enculturation achieved? Students began primary studies around the age of seven, first learning the "three R's" and then coming under the tutelage of a *grammatikos*, a teacher of grammar.

7. M. L. Clarke, *Higher Education in the Ancient World* (London: Routledge & K. Paul, 1971), p. 2.

8. Clarke, p. 11.

9. Clarke, p. 2.

10. Stanley F. Bonner, *Education in Ancient Rome* (Berkeley: U of CA Press, 1977), p. xi.

11. R. R. Bolgar quoted in Simmons, p. 80.

12. Simmons, p. 73; cf. also Clarke, p. 14.

By grammar, the ancients meant more than just language mechanics or parts of speech. Grammar included the study of the great literary works of the culture. Dionysius Thrax, who authored the first Greek grammar textbook, defined grammar as "the practical knowledge of the ways of poets and prose writers," which included six parts:

> reading with correct pronunciation; explanation of poetic figures of speech; explanation of rare words and of the subject matter; etymology; analogy (that is, the doctrine of regular grammatical forms); and the criticism of poetry.[13]

Among the great works studied, Homer took pride of place, and every schoolboy committed huge chunks of his works to memory.[14] Drama and lyric poetry were also studied.[15] A typical day in a grammar school would include recitation of the previous day's work; copying and reading aloud a set passage from a book; listening to and taking notes on the master's explanation of the passage; sight reading; recitation of memorized lists of nouns or lines of verse; discussions of grammatical points; dictation and more reading aloud.[16] The key was to hold before the students "the habitual vision of greatness"—the very best the culture had to offer.[17]

Other subjects included the Quadrivium or mathematical arts: arithmetic, geometry, astronomy, and music. Basic arithmetic facts would have been part of general education, although we have little direct evidence on the subject. Romans might employ a *calculator*, an instructor who taught what would today be called "business math,"[18] but these studies would have been distinct from the more elevated liberal arts.[19] In

---

13. Clarke, p. 13.
14. Clarke, p. 18, p. 20.
15. Clarke, pp. 18-19.
16. Clarke, p. 27.
17. Simmons, p. 45.
18. Clarke, p. 46.
19. Clarke, p. 47.

the latter context, mathematics provided not practical skills alone but also mental training or preparation for philosophy.[20] "Arithmetic meant the theory of numbers. Geometry...start[ed] with definition and, after setting out certain postulates and axioms, proceed[ed] to prove a series of theorems."[21] Astronomy, a popular study, was approached with introductory textbooks and definitions.[22] Topics might include learning "constellations; the Milky Way, the tropics, the equator and the ecliptic; the rising and settings of the stars; and finally weather signs." Planetary movements were studied in a more advanced course.[23] Music was lauded as a moral study by Plato and was a regular part of Greek civic and religious life, and thus, of education. While vocal and instrumental instruction did continue both in Greece and in Rome, music came to be treated as a theoretical and mathematical subject. Perhaps we might best understand it as the scientific study of harmonics and music theory. So, for example, schools of music might provide for study of intervals, scales, and the modes.[24] Still, the moral character of practical musical education persisted. A text attributed to Plutarch declares:

> If a man has diligently studied music as part of education and has given it the necessary attention in early years, he will commend and embrace what is noble and condemn what is not, in music and in other matters too; and one so educated will be free from all ignoble action and, reaping the greatest benefit from music, he will prove of the highest value to himself and his city, since all his actions and words will be well tempered and always and everywhere he will maintain a sense of fitness, self-control and orderliness.[25]

20. Clarke, p. 46.
21. Clarke, p. 49.
22. Clarke, pp. 50-51.
23. Clarke, p. 51.
24. Clarke, pp. 52-54.
25. Quoted in Clarke, p. 54.

After the basics of elementary education, the student might continue on to a school of rhetoric where he would be trained to write and speak correctly and persuasively. Rhetorical training would begin, sometimes in the grammar years, with the *progymnasmata*, a graded series of written exercises that came before the speeches that formed the core of the work in schools of rhetoric.[26] The goal of these exercises

> was not so much to encourage imagination and powers of independent thought as to develop in the learner a command of the resources of language, an ability to say the same thing in a number of different ways. The schoolboy learned not to express his own feelings and experience but to elaborate and adorn his theme on accepted lines, to paraphrase, for instance, a moral maxim and support it by simile, example and quotation.[27]

From the ages of fifteen to eighteen or so, students might attend the lectures of various rhetoric teachers.[28] Rhetorical study consisted of both theory and practice. The former might be outlined in textbooks or lectures.[29] The latter would be pursued through two kinds of declamation: the *suasoria* and the *controversia*. In the *suasoria*, the student composed a speech giving advice to some historical person at a crucial turning point; the *controversia* were speeches imitating those of the law courts.[30]

A typical approach to the themes was as follows: The teacher, having announced the theme, analyzed it in a lecture known as the *divisio, praelocutio,* or *praefatio* (*protheoria* in Greek). Next he stood and delivered a declamation on the topic while students listened and perhaps took notes. Students then performed their own compositions, first reading aloud while seated, then more formally, standing, and from memory. Finally,

---

26. Clarke, p. 25.
27. Clarke, p. 38.
28. Clarke, p. 33.
29. Clarke, pp. 34-35.
30. Clarke, p. 39.

the teacher critiqued their performance.[31]

After completing his rhetorical studies, a talented student might continue on to more advanced studies, such as higher mathematics and philosophy. Some histories might be read in the Greek schools as part of rhetoric, but history was not considered a subject of study in its own right.[32] Likewise, science and logic were largely philosophical disciplines and were studied, if at all, after a boy had finished his general education. A boy might also go through a period of physical training in preparation for military service.[32]

The Medieval Schools: The Classical Inheritance Redeemed

With the fall of Rome propelling Western Europe into the Dark Ages, the Church became a lifeboat for classical culture and learning. The Church did not deem everything she inherited of equal value: The early Church fathers grappled with the demands of their faith and the lure of worldly learning. But the learning survived, and "[t]he curriculum fixed in antiquity remained unchallenged so far as concerned the liberal arts."[33]

> Religious faith was gradually joined, if shakily, to classical learning. Slowly were Christians integrated back into pagan culture, not to be reclaimed by paganism, but to reap the best that classical culture had sown. Christians christened the classical heritage.[34]

This integration, articulated by Boethius in the early Middle Ages, reached its zenith with Thomas Aquinas's magisterial attempt to reconcile

31. Clarke, pp. 42-43.
32. Clarke, p. 21.
33. Clarke, p. 141.
34. Simmons, p. 86.

Christian theology and Aristotelian logic, the *Summa Theologica.*[35]

The adaptation of Latin to the rigors of medieval theology and law did not leave the language unchanged. In the mouths of the Scholastics, Latin often became crabbed and jargon-laden, lacking the refinement of the classical tongue. It continued to be taught and learned for the simple reason that it was the language of the Church and of the educated elite:

> Thus in the Middle Ages, Latin was made the groundwork of education; not for the beauty of its classical literature, nor because the study of a dead language was the best mental gymnastic, or the only means of acquiring a masterly freedom in the use of living tongues, but because it was the language of educated men throughout Europe, employed for public business, literature, philosophy, and science....[36]

In addition to the continued cultivation of Latin in grammar textbooks like that of Donatus, the ancient Quadrivium gained importance as Greek ideas re-entered the West by way of Arabic sources. Finally, the medieval system gave birth both to the universities and to flourishing vernacular literatures in French, Italian, German, Spanish, and English.

Although logic appears among the medieval Trivium subjects, it was, as in the ancient world, linked to the study of philosophy, and, in the medieval context, with theology.[37] In fact, logic came to eclipse other studies. "From about the middle of the twelfth century logic became the all-absorbing interest of the schools and ousted the humanistic studies represented by grammar and rhetoric."[38] And later: "The prevailing passion for logic and the rediscovery of the complete Aristotle led to neglect not only of grammar and rhetoric but also of the quadrivium."[39] By the

---

35. Clarke, pp. 139-140.
36. Quoted in Simmons, pp. 88-89.
37. Clarke, pp. 4-5.
38. Clarke, p. 142.
39. Clarke, p. 143.

late Middle Ages, literary studies were severely truncated, with grammar school ending at the age of fourteen and few, if any, classical Latin texts studied. Grammar and literature were moving apart into the distinct subjects we know today.[40]

Logic was studied less for its own sake than as a handmaid to law and theology. As Abelard, one of the primary architects of the new, reason-based theology explained,

> If believers are allowed to read works on the liberal arts and the books of the ancients it is…that we may be able to grasp whatever concerns the understanding or the beauty of Holy Scripture, or the defence and support of its truth.[41]

Logic also led directly into philosophy, particularly that of Aristotle, whose works formed almost the whole of the philosophical curriculum in this period.[42]

Mathematics was not wholly neglected. In fact, the reception of mathematical ideas from Arabic sources supported advances in the field, especially beginning in the twelfth century. By the late Middle Ages, Euclid was being studied in the universities of both northern and southern Europe.[43]

In sum, the liberal arts in the medieval period carried on the classical heritage primarily in its Greek form. Although we often associate the revival of Greek ideals with the Renaissance, historian M. L. Clarke reminds us that medieval education, despite its reliance on the Latin language,

> was essentially Greek in character. The curriculum was that of the Greek schools of later antiquity, and the scholastic philosophers

---

40. Clarke, p. 145.
41. Quoted in Clarke, p. 142.
42. Clarke, p. 148.
43. Clarke, p. 147.

with their love of subtle dialectic argument are more Greek than
Roman.[44]

Renaissance Revival: Style as Substance

The Renaissance was, in turn, in many ways a return to Roman
educational ideals, including the bilingual *doctrina duplex* that again
became normative for classical education during this period.[45]

If medieval Latin was all content and no form, the Renaissance re-
introduced a concern for substantial thought conveyed stylishly. Greek
was taught once again, and the emphasis was on the best possible models
for thought and expression. Like their ancient role models, the Renaissance humanists adhered to the principle of *multum non multa*—not
many, but much. If "style was the obvious mark of the educated man,"[46]
then only the best literary works were to be studied. Still, the number of
subjects multiplied to include history, ethics, and poetry.

The goal of this devotion to the classical inheritance was unabashedly moral. Education should ennoble. So, for example, "[o]ne read of
great men to glean examples of upright living and noble deeds; one read
of evil men in order to learn from their evil deeds what the good man or
woman must avoid."[47]

In Latin, students read Virgil, Lucan, Horace, Juvenal, Ovid, Cicero, Plautus, and Terence. In Greek, they read Thucydides, Xenophon,
Herodotus, Ptolemy, Strabo, and above all, Plutarch. Plato and Aristotle
were rarely read, and the works of the great Athenian playwrights were
unknown.[48] Models for composition came directly from the ancients, especially Cicero, who was lauded as *unus scribendi magister*, "the one and

---

44. Clarke, p. 151.
45. Clarke, p. 151.
46. Simmons, p. 95.
47. Simmons, p. 101.
48. Simmons, pp. 102-103.

only teacher of writing."[49] The Northern Christian humanist Erasmus had strong ideas about reading as well. In addition to the writers favored in Italy, he insisted on Aesop for beginners, Euripides, Aristophanes, Lucian, and Demosthenes in Greek; and Seneca, Sallust, and Quintilian in Latin. Christian writers such as Jerome and Augustine rounded out the curriculum.

The sixteenth century saw the humanistic curriculum become entrenched in Britain, where Latin might even be taught by the "direct approach," that is, conversationally, as a spoken language.[50] By the following century—the time of the great English poets Donne, Milton, and Dryden—classical learning was the norm. It is from this period that we get the term "grammar school," meaning a school in which Greek and Latin, not English, were taught.[51] English was, in fact, little taught at all, a fact that might puzzle us when we consider the tremendous outpouring of mature English literature of the period. But the people of the time would not have been surprised: "[...] the brightest minds thought that mastery with English—or at least mastery with English of the best kind—came by way of classical training."[52]

That training was rigorous in the extreme:

> Students might, for example, be made to translate a Greek verse into clean English prose and then into Latin verse. Variations were entertained freely, the harder—and more apparently nonsensical—the workouts the better. The aim of all these exercises was never merely to learn the languages and the literatures of the Greeks and Romans. Their value was not merely cultural. The point of this method was to stretch students' minds, to expand their capacities, to inure them to manipulating, to playing with, words and ideas. A literary high culture would have no need to

49. Simmons, p. 105.
50. Simmons, p. 114.
51. Simmons, p. 121.
52. Simmons, p. 123.

justify this flagrant expenditure of its students' time and effort. These students were novices. They were not learning a trade; they were improving their mental natures.[53]

Educating for Enlightenment: Tradition and Innovation

It was out of this elevated intellectual milieu that the eighteenth-century American Founders emerged. Not all of the Founders were classically educated—George Washington, notably, was not—but they still lived and breathed classical culture. Their assumed definitions of an educated man can be divined from the entrance requirements to the New World colleges:

> When any scholar is able to read Tully [Cicero] or such like classical Latin Author extempore, and make and speak true Latin in verse and prose…without any assistance whatever and decline perfectly the paradigms of nouns and verbs in the Greek tongue, then may he be admitted into the College, nor shall any claim admission before such qualification.

So read the requirements for matriculation at Harvard in 1642. King's College (later Columbia University) required only Greek, Latin, and arithmetic.[54] In eighteenth-century Britain, the principle of *multum non multa* still applied: "[t]he aim became one of reading—and re-reading—a few masterpieces rather than many. It was better to be thorough than broad in one's classical reading."[55]

The following century saw a further codification of the classical curriculum in the great British public schools. Training began, as it had for the ancients, with memorization, both of grammatical forms and of

---

53. Simmons, p. 124.

54. Simmons, p. 132.

55. Simmons, p. 127.

the great poets.[56] Composition in prose and especially verse—a remnant of Renaissance educational methods—formed the best and brightest minds of the British Empire.[57] The great scholars and teachers of the time recognized that classical study enriched society, and that great nations require great leaders:

> Thomas Arnold [nineteenth-century headmaster of Rugby] would write in the preface of his edition of Thucydides that his effort was "not an idle inquiry about remote ages and forgotten institutions but a living picture of things present, fitted not so much for the curiosity of the scholar as for the instruction of the statesman and the citizen."[58]

Victorian England saw the spread of classical models down from the public schools to less august institutions. Yet along with this popularization came the institutionalization of classical education, which was increasingly seen as the purview of scholars and specialists.

Goodbye, Mr. Chips: The Decline of Classical Education

Only a few years after Queen Victoria's death, the last generation of classically educated Englishmen would be dying on the fields of France in the Great War. The post-war years saw rising demand for practical, commercial skills, and this trend only increased after World War II with the G.I. Bill in the United States. Despite a number of spirited apologies from men like T. S. Eliot and Albert Jay Nock, classical education was swept away by the modernist theories of John Dewey.

Thus we enter the era of what Russell Kirk called "Behemoth U.," the university as vocational training center, offering a smattering of courses

---

56. Simmons, p. 129.
57. Simmons, p. 129-130.
58. Simmons, p. 136.

leading to a degree but not to knowledge, let alone wisdom. While the WW II generation might still have benefited from the remaining shadows of the classical model—Wheelock's Latin text was written for returning G.I.'s—by the time their children reached high school in the 1960s, Latin had all but disappeared from the schools.

Dorothy Sayers and the Reinvention of the Trivium

But even in the post-war years, classical education had not lost all its defenders. In a speech at Oxford in 1947, scholar, playwright, and novelist Dorothy Sayers took up the cause. She explained to her audience of educators that, while she was not an expert in the field of pedagogy, she did have the useful perspective of a medievalist. Drawing on her knowledge of medieval education, she proposed to take the Trivium as a model for modern education.

The syllabus of the medieval schools, she explained,

> ...was divided into two parts: the Trivium and Quadrivium. The second part—the Quadrivium—consisted of "subjects," and need not for the moment concern us. The interesting thing for us is the composition of the Trivium, which preceded the Quadrivium and was the preliminary discipline for it. It consisted of three parts: Grammar, Dialectic, and Rhetoric, in that order.

Each of these is both a subject—"at that period [Grammar] meant learning Latin," said Sayers—and an approach to language itself:

> The whole of the Trivium was, in fact, intended to teach the pupil the proper use of the tools of learning, before he began to apply them to "subjects" at all. First, he learned a language; not just how to order a meal in a foreign language, but the structure of a

language, and hence of language itself—what it was, how it was put together, and how it worked. Secondly, he learned how to use language; how to define his terms and make accurate statements; how to construct an argument and how to detect fallacies in argument. Dialectic, that is to say, embraced Logic and Disputation. Thirdly, he learned to express himself in language—how to say what he had to say elegantly and persuasively.

In Sayers' model, then, the Trivium is understood, not as the *content* of specific subjects, but as descriptive of *stages* of intellectual development. In a much-quoted passage, she went on to describe how these stages apply to modern children:

The Poll-Parrot stage is the one in which learning by heart is easy and, on the whole, pleasurable; whereas reasoning is difficult and, on the whole, little relished. At this age, one readily memorizes the shapes and appearances of things; one likes to recite the number-plates of cars; one rejoices in the chanting of rhymes and the rumble and thunder of unintelligible polysyllables; one enjoys the mere accumulation of things. The Pert age, which follows upon this (and, naturally, overlaps it to some extent), is characterized by contradicting, answering back, liking to "catch people out" (especially one's elders); and by the propounding of conundrums. Its nuisance-value is extremely high. It usually sets in about the Fourth Form. The Poetic age is popularly known as the "difficult" age. It is self-centered; it yearns to express itself; it rather specializes in being misunderstood; it is restless and tries to achieve independence; and, with good luck and good guidance, it should show the beginnings of creativeness; a reaching out towards a synthesis of what it already knows, and a deliberate eagerness to know and do some one thing in preference to all others. Now it seems to me that the layout of the Trivium adapts itself with a singular appropriateness to these three ages: Grammar to the Poll-Parrot, Dialectic to the Pert, and Rhetoric to the Poetic age.

Sayers suggested that, in each stage, the bulk of the student's time and effort be devoted to the appropriate Trivium subject. Regarding the elementary-school Poll-Parrot stage, for example, Sayers stated, "I will say at once, quite firmly, that the best grounding for education is the Latin grammar." (As we will see, some of Sayers' popularizers have made surprisingly little of this directive.) Logic will be the focus of the Pert stage (roughly the middle school or junior high years) and, Rhetoric, in turn, will receive the emphasis in the Poetic high school years.

Sayers further observed that each subject has its own internal grammar, logic, and rhetoric. The grammar of a subject consists of essential facts and rules: "The grammar of History should consist, I think, of dates, events, anecdotes, and personalities." The logic of a subject encompasses the relationships between the facts and rules, which can be determined analytically. The rhetoric of a subject, then, culminates in the clear expression and creative application of the material grasped and analyzed in the previous two stages. Facts, analysis, synthesis: The Trivium becomes a methodology for approaching any subject. Sayers writes:

> Once again, the contents of the syllabus at this stage may be anything you like. The "subjects" supply material; but they are all to be regarded as mere grist for the mental mill to work upon.

This last aspect of Sayers' applied Trivium, promoted by Douglas Wilson and his colleagues in the Association of Classical and Christian Schools, has seen great acceptance by Christian classical educators.[59] Sayers' three-stage model has also been widely adopted by home schoolers, popularized particularly by Susan Wise Bauer and Jessie Wise in their best-selling guide, *The Well-Trained Mind*. Bauer and Wise promote a

---

59. Gene Edward Veith, Jr. and Andrew Kern, *Classical Education: The Movement Sweeping America* (Washington, DC: Capital Research Center, 2001), pp. 19-22.

rigorous, language-based (as opposed to "image-based") education, culminating in the study of the Great Books. While they strongly recommend the study of Latin and make a good case for its importance as part of a classical education, they deny Latin its historical position at the center of the classical curriculum. Instead, they state, "Latin is not the defining element of a classical education."[60]

Toward a Definition of Classical Education

As we have seen, for over two thousand years—indeed, until less than a century ago—"classical education" meant one thing and one thing only: training in the classical languages and immersion in classical culture. Tracy Lee Simmons writes:

> Once classical education pointed to an elite course of instruction based upon Greek and Latin, the two great languages of the classical world. But it also delved into the history, philosophy, literature, and art of the Greek and Roman worlds, affording over time to the more perspicacious devotees a remarkably high degree of cultural understanding, an understanding that endured and marked the learner for life. Classical education was classical immersion.[61]

Bauer seems less concerned with historical definitions:

> [Y]ou should always remember that everyone who does classical education (including Charlotte Mason, the Bluedorns, Doug Wilson, Christine Miller, and ourselves) is adapting an old model to a modern context. In effect, we're all "neoclassical" educators, modifying, improving (we hope) and changing the ancient ways of

60. Susan Wise Bauer and Jessie Wise, *The Well-Trained Mind*, rev. ed. (New York: Norton, 2003), p. 190.

61. Simmons, p. 13.

learning so that they make sense for students today. None of these adaptations are "straight from Plato's mouth," which makes arguments about the "genuine classical" method somewhat pointless.[62]

It is certainly true that all twenty-first-century educators must, can, and do adapt the historical models of the ancient and medieval worlds to modern circumstances. This book does that no less than any other. Yet, as Plato would have affirmed, we do need a definition within this context since "classical" is used so broadly in society. Proponents of traditional classical education might well point out that, in following Sayers, neoclassical educators have not just adapted classical education to present needs—they have *fundamentally redefined* it, and in the process, altered the very core of the approach. Simmons writes:

> Today we use the term licentiously. We apply "classic" or "classical" to anything we believe to be excellent and universal. [...] Thus nowadays may classical education refer to something not linked to the classical world at all—never mind the languages—and get equated with what might once have been called simply traditional or orthodox education. [...] And now legions of well-intending home schoolers rush to put dibs on the term and bask in the light of the glory they believe it to exude. [...] I will only say to all these good people that extending "classical" to mark an approach or course of study without reference to Greek and Latin seems an unnecessarily promiscuous usage.[63]

"Can someone be 'classically educated' without a reading knowledge of Greek and Latin?" asks Simmons.

This sticky question, despite dogmatic claims on both sides, should not be answered glibly. One must probe a little to discover

---

62. Susan Wise Bauer, "Charlotte Mason and Classical Education," http://www.welltrainedmind.com/charlottemason.php, viewed 11/19/04.

63. Simmons, pp. 14-15.

precisely what kind of knowledge the questioner wishes to gain. The judgment of history is No.[64]

Where does this leave us? First, it should be understood that, arguments about definitions aside, the educational model proposed by writers like Bauer and Wise, the Bluedorns, Douglas Wilson, and others is an excellent one. It will not do to denigrate educators who are "repairing the ruins" of the liberal arts, to use Wilson's apt phrase. A rigorous education in the humanities, with its broad reading and engagement in the Great Conversation, is nothing to scoff at, and any amount of Latin is better than none. We could do—and for almost a century our public schools have done—far worse.

If we should not diminish the laudable efforts of our fellow educators, neither should we fail to acknowledge the considerable common ground that exists between the traditional classical and neoclassical models. Many neoclassical educators do encourage the study of Latin, and to a lesser extent, Greek. They do take seriously the study of logic and rhetoric as subjects in themselves. They do take pains to familiarize their students with the riches of the ancient world through Great Books programs and a thorough grounding in world history. All of this is perfectly in accord with the traditional model, and we will explore some of these commonalities in the rest of this book.

Further, we must acknowledge that Dorothy Sayers' insights into child development are shored up by the practical experience of generations of teachers of all sorts; the Poll-Parrot, Pert, and Poetic stages are readily observable in our classrooms and around our kitchen tables. While I am wary of the tendency to fetishize educational "ages and stages," I would not go so far as to deny entirely the validity of Sayers' approach. Quite simply, it appears to work.

Finally, I admit that in attempting to return to an historical understanding of classical education, I am fighting a losing battle. The Sayers

---

64. Simmons, p. 26.

Trivium is too entrenched in our consciousness to be overthrown by a few raving Latinists. However, as a healthy respect for the past is common to all types of classical educators, I will nevertheless make my plea that we repent of the linguistic promiscuity for which Simmons takes us to task. In that spirit, and with all due respect to others whose definitions differ, when the term "classical education" is used in this book, it will refer exclusively to the traditional, Latin- and/or Greek-based curriculum as described by Simmons in *Climbing Parnassus* and promoted among contemporary home schoolers by Cheryl Lowe of Memoria Press and the Highlands Latin School, among others.

We are now able to endorse a definition of classical education, proposed by Tracy Lee Simmons, that not only rests on the firm foundation of history but that also points the way to contemporary application. This definition does not attempt to say what the goals of a classical education might be or what sort of person it might produce; I trust the preceding survey has given the reader some sense of that, and the next chapter will examine those questions in greater detail. Rather, this definition merely states what a classical education consists of "on the ground."

> **[Classical education is] a curriculum grounded upon—if not strictly limited to—Greek, Latin, and the study of the civilization from which they arose.** [65]

---

65. Simmons, p. 15.

II. WHY LATIN AND GREEK?

To lose what I owe to Plato and Aristotle would be like the amputation of a limb. Hardly any lawful price would seem to me too high for what I have gained by being made to learn Latin and Greek. —**C. S. Lewis**

ꐦ

The *doctrina duplex*—the study of the ancient languages and literatures of both Greece and Rome—has clearly stood the test of time. Why? What is it about this particular curriculum that makes it worth the considerable time and trouble necessary for students to master it?

Arguments in favor of a Latin- and Greek-based curriculum fall into three main categories. Here we'll deal with each category separately, although there is some overlap.

Utilitarian Arguments

The ancients did not press practical arguments too far, for as Aristotle said, "To seek utility everywhere is most unsuitable to lofty and free natures."[66] Yet these are the benefits of classical education that we pragmatic moderns are likely to point to first. They also answer some of the common objections that skeptical family and friends may have about your educational choices.

1. *Knowledge of classical languages increases English vocabulary.* Approximately half of the vocabulary of English comes from Latin roots and another twenty percent from Greek. These words tend to be the difficult, polysyllabic ones—"SAT words." A thorough knowledge of classical languages will increase the student's English vocabulary tremendously.

---

66. Quoted in Simmons, p. 215.

2. *Classical languages aid in the understanding of English grammar.* Studying a highly inflected language—that is, one that marks grammatical changes with a fully developed system of case endings—gives students a better grasp of English grammar. In fact, generations of teachers have observed that Latin teaches English better than English![67]

3. *Latin is the key to the modern Romance languages.* Knowing Latin makes it much easier to learn the grammar and vocabulary of the modern Romance languages (e.g., Spanish, French, Italian, Portuguese, Romanian), since they derive eighty percent or more of their vocabulary from Latin. Both classical tongues greatly aid in learning other inflected languages, such as German or Russian.

4. *Latin students perform exceptionally well on standardized tests and are sought after by competitive colleges.* As a result of increased vocabulary and facility with English grammar, students of Latin consistently outperform their peers—including those who have studied modern languages—on the verbal portion of the SATs. Between 1997 and 2004, Latin students outscored the average by *157 points.* Higher scores open doors to competitive colleges and scholarships such as the National Merit program.

5. *Some careers require knowledge of classical languages.* The technical vocabulary of the medical and legal professions and the hard sciences rests on the foundation of Latin and Greek. Latin is still a required subject for some higher degrees, as is Greek for many entering the ministry.

---

67. Cheryl Lowe, *Classical Teacher*, Winter 2003, p. 3.

Cultural Arguments

While the ancients did not emphasize utilitarian arguments in defending or explaining their educational system, they did argue for it on cultural grounds. Ancient education meant *enculturation*, the process by which the highest values of their societies were passed on to the next generation. This is as necessary for us as it was for them—perhaps more so, in this age of relativism and anti-intellectualism.

1. *Knowledge of the classics increases cultural literacy.* Just as Latin increases literacy in English, so does familiarity with Graeco-Roman culture increase cultural literacy. Along with the Bible, classical literature is the key to understanding English literature, as well as the literatures of Europe (e.g., Dante, English Romantic poets). Likewise, art and music are studded with classical references (e.g., Botticelli's *Venus*, Handel's *Semele*).

2. *Classical history is our history.* As Westerners, we are all heirs to the cultural patrimony of Greece and Rome. Familiarity with the history of the classical world helps in understanding the foundations of modern democratic government.

3. *The cultural experience of the ancient world is highly relevant to us today.* The Roman Empire has been called the first great multiethnic society. Study of Roman successes and failures in this area is timely. Likewise, someone who is familiar with ancient warfare will have a useful perspective on more recent military conflicts.[68]

---

68. Cf. David V. Hicks, *Norms and Nobility* (Savage: MD: Rowman & Littlefield, 1991), p. 11.

Formative Arguments

The classical curriculum has an unsurpassed track record, not just in filling students' minds with useful knowledge, but also in *forming* their minds and their spirits. Intellectual discipline, moral virtue, and appreciation of beauty are the regular results of running the classical race.

1. *The classical curriculum imparts exceptional intellectual discipline.* Classical languages form the mind, inculcating the habits of precision and attention to detail. "Every lesson in Latin is a lesson in logic."[69] Intellectual rigor prepares the student to discern what is True. It is the surest remedy for the modern ill of relativism.

2. *The classical curriculum inspires moral insight and virtue.* The classical world first codified the great virtues of prudence, temperance, justice, and courage. Keeping before the student "the habitual vision of greatness" inspires and uplifts the mind and spirit toward the Good.

3. *The classical curriculum forms aesthetic judgment.* Just as the vision of greatness inspires us in the moral realm, living in constant contact with the highest artistic achievements of the West cultivates a taste for the Beautiful. In time, the student will not just appreciate his culture, but will be able to emulate its best and brightest.

Home schooling parents cite many of these reasons when they explain why they have chosen a traditional classical curriculum. Here is how some classical home schoolers explain their educational choices.

---

69. Simmons, p. 177.

I've chosen this kind of education for my children because it has stood the test of time. Sometimes I think children in government schools (and even some private schools) are guinea pigs for the many experimental programs generated by the universities that train teachers. And their methods seem to provide nothing more than mediocrity. I just don't believe that we, as a society, are as well-educated as those who have come before us. [...] [I]t seems that even the lesser-educated people in the earlier days of our country (USA) knew more and understood more than some college-educated folks today. So I have turned to a more classical approach in an attempt to provide a simpler, more traditional form of education for my children.
Amy H., Virginia, USA

I chose it because a mind that has been asked to follow a rigourous learning plan is never out-of-date. My goal as an educator is to equip my students with the tools they need in order to learn whatever it is they want to do in life, whether it's how to work a washing machine or draft architectural drawings. I believe that with a classical education my children will have the mental equivalent of a gymnast's body—strong, flexible, well-honed, practiced. **Sarah Schira, Manitoba, Canada**

Last weekend I attended a Home School Curriculum Resources Day in Cambridge, England, and afterwards was invited for a meal in the home of a Botanical Science researcher, who also does some teaching at the University. The conversation turned to the current standard of education. He remarked that during his twelve years in Cambridge the standard of applicants for the field in which he does his research and teaches had fallen each year. He told me standards had fallen to such an extent this year, [that] if during the interview process he had 'held' to their standard, *none of the interviewed candidates would have been accepted* into the course. Standards, this lecturer told me, had plummeted since Cambridge and Oxford and had removed…pre-requisites… in Latin and Greek language. For me it is indeed time to return to the tried and proven methods of earlier times. **Peter McGrath, Ireland**

My ultimate goal is to teach my children to think for themselves, not just to memorize facts for a test. Memorizing facts is how I was taught. I know a lot of miscellaneous info, but I don't know how to apply it all of the time. I want my boys to be able to look at any statement and (1) consider it logically, (2) discern whether or not it is valid, and (3) articulate their point of view. **Beth L. Saathoff, Texas, USA**

The bottom line for most parents is, "Does it work?" Does this form of education have a proven track record of producing people who can navigate through life successfully and, indeed, excel? Do these people exhibit high levels of virtue and wisdom, or at least recognize those qualities—and their opposites—for what they are? Given that virtually all of the movers and shakers of our culture until about a hundred years ago were educated this way, I think we can answer that question with an unqualified yes. Can we do the same for other forms of education? Not to the same degree.

Pro and Contra:
Seven Objections to the Study of Latin and Greek

Why, if the classical curriculum was so successful, was it summarily discarded about a century ago? The answer to that question involves political, social, and economic factors too complex to explore here.[70] In fact, the modernist educational ideas championed by twentieth-century progressives are now so entrenched in our minds—and our schools—that we hardly know *how* to question them. Worse, in recent years we have left behind even the optimistic progressivism of the moderns and adopted the inchoate relativism of post-modernism, with its rejection of "unifying metanarratives" and deconstruction of language and truth itself.[71]

In our cultural moment, the prospects for classical education seem bleak indeed. The naysayers are many. How can we respond to some typical objections to the classical curriculum?

Just as the most accessible arguments for classical education are based on utilitarian assumptions—a bias formed, it must be admitted, by our own impoverished educational and intellectual environment—so are the first five objections to it.

1. *The study of classical languages and cultures wastes precious time that could be more profitably spent learning practical skills (e.g., computers).*

Intellectual training is never wasted. Those who are trained today for technical careers often find that their skills are outmoded before they ever finish their course of study, let alone find a job. Students with classical training have the ability to learn virtually any technical skill quickly and efficiently—and they also have the

---

70. For an enlightening study of the history of progressive educational reform in the United States, see Diane Ravitch, *Left Back: A Century of Failed School Reforms* (New York: Simon & Schuster, 2000). For the devastating effects of those reforms on the public schools and universities, see Thomas Sowell, *Inside American Education* (New York: Free Press, 1993).

71. Veith & Kern, pp. 1-4.

wisdom to ask how that skill can best be applied. In the words of John Henry Newman, liberal learning teaches the student

> [t]o see things as they are, to go right to the point, to disentangle a skein of thought, to detect what is sophistical, and to discard what is irrelevant. It prepares him to fill any post with credit, and to master any subject with facility.[72]

2. *The same cultural literacy and expansive vocabulary can be achieved through a combination of broad English reading—perhaps including Classics in translation—and the judicious use of reference works, scholarly footnotes, and annotated editions.*

While it is certainly true that Latinless students can excel in English, they cannot hope to plumb the real depths of classical literature in translation. As Simmons notes, "The problem with translations is that those readers unlettered in the original languages can't know what they're missing."[73] A Japanese reading a translation of Shakespeare can accurately recount the plot of "Hamlet," but can he be said to understand the play's artistry without having experienced Shakespeare's own language? Likewise, memorizing a list of classical roots or common Latin phrases is useful as far as it goes; but it does not go far enough. It cannot supply the original context for this information. Despite the laudable efforts of the Core Knowledge Foundation, classical references learned out of context—"Oedipus complex," "Achilles' heel," "crossing the Rubicon"—remain little more than intellectual trivia. The classical student's knowledge is, in contrast, contextualized and can therefore be used with confidence and skill:

---

72. Quoted in Hicks, p. 127.
73. Simmons, p. 218.

The modest weight of learning we drag along prevents us from being racked, as are some of our fellows, with an anxiety to look smart. We don't listen in our cars to cassette programs designed to increase our vocabulary—the vocabulary we learned neither at home nor at school—while we're trapped in rush hours in order to beat the competition in a corporate meeting with new, spiffy words. Our apprenticeship has already been served, though it doesn't inspire smugness.[74]

3. *Latin is hard and boring; it's too dull and irrelevant for students to enjoy.*

The Roman orator Quintilian, who evidently faced similar excuses, minces no words on this subject: "The excuse of 'difficulty' is a cloak for our idleness." Anything worth achieving takes time and hard work. Many people profess to dislike math, but no sensible educator would therefore argue that we should simply drop it from the curriculum. We should not confuse challenge with tedium, or unimaginative teaching with a dull subject.

4. *Some people just aren't good at languages; their minds don't work that way, and it's a waste of time to force them into something they'll never learn well.*

Most often this objection comes from intelligent adults who themselves made a poor showing at one or another foreign language. In my experience as a language teacher, I have found that virtually all of these people were suffering from one lack: poor teaching. If you can speak, read, and write your native tongue—in other words, if you are of normal intelligence—you can become competent in a foreign language. Yes, even a "hard" one like Latin.

---

74. Simmons, p. 169.

5. *But some people don't have "normal intelligence"—what about learning disabilities?*

We must be realistic here: The potential for success in Latin—and therefore, in a traditional classical curriculum—does depend to a certain extent on natural ability. A severely mentally handicapped person is an unlikely candidate for a classical education. But "normal intelligence" does not mean a stratospheric IQ, and children with some of the more common auditory or phonological processing problems may still do well in Latin. According to Barbara Hill, Coordinator of the Latin program at the University of Colorado, Boulder, "[r]ecent research suggests that Latin is a viable choice for students with learning problems."[75]

This concern leads us to the first political objection, which takes exception to any form of education that is not universally accessible.

6. *Classical education is elitist and therefore unsuitable for a democratic society.*

If excellence is undemocratic, then classical education is guilty as charged. It is unabashedly meritocratic, lifting up the best above the rest. And this is what makes it of the greatest use to a forward-looking society. No society can flourish without the constant stimulation of great minds driving it on. Our society shows the degrading effects of systematically quashing excellence and neglecting the nurture of the finest minds. We should not diminish our commitments to democracy and freedom by poisoning them with intellectual envy. At the heart of the mainstream dumbed-down curriculum is the invidious assumption that "if everyone can't excel, no one should."

At the same time, we must recognize that, in a prosperous, democratic nation, access to a rigorous education with high, ennobling

---

75. Barbara Hill, "Latin for Students with Learning Disabilities" (CAMWS Committee for the Promotion of Latin, http://www.camwscpl.org). A leaflet with select bibliography is available for download at http://www.promotelatin.org/LatinforLDbrochure.pdf

standards need not be limited to the wealthy. Rather, a true commitment to democracy would dictate that *all* citizens be given the opportunity to run the classical race. While there are no guarantees that all will achieve equal success—common sense tells us as much—the example of inner-city classical academies like Westside Preparatory Academy in Chicago shows that poverty or a difficult home life need not be a barrier to academic excellence. Acclaimed school founder Marva Collins states unequivocally, "Low expectations [are] a sin."[76]

> Marva Collins' curriculum emphasizes reasoning skills. She takes offense that she should do otherwise than teach liberal studies courses; mere vocational training will not lift students out of their social conditions. Of course, she recognizes that education generally increases earnings, but she insists that money is neither the sole means to education nor its end. A child of the ghetto needs a liberal education precisely because it provides choices that vocational training cannot. The goal is [...] freedom.[77]

A variation on the elitism accusation, most often voiced by Christian parents, is that classically educated students will become arrogant or "puffed up" with secular knowledge. While I do not in any way wish to suggest that we ignore the clear warnings of Scripture, I do not think that classical education, in itself, is more likely to lead to intellectual arrogance than any other type of schooling. It is certainly possible for any accomplished student to lord it over his peers, but a classically educated student might just as well echo Socrates in admitting how little he really knows. Christians, in particular, are given divine insight into the limits of human philosophy from the perspective of eternity. Who among us can answer the questions posed in Job 38 with anything but reverent silence?

76. Veith & Kern, p. 50.
77. Veith & Kern, p. 51.

7. *Classical education is too focused on Western culture and is therefore unsuitable for our multicultural society and may even be racist in its assumptions and approach.*

Often this objection is predicated on a simple misunderstanding about the content of a classical education, based on the admittedly imperfect terms "Latin-centered" or "Latin-based." As will be clear from what follows, classical education indeed places classical languages and cultures at the center of the curriculum, but not to the total exclusion of other subjects. Rather, all subjects are related back to the core classical ones. Information about other cultures is conveyed through the subjects of literature, history, and geography—which, long before the advent of "social studies," included not just desultory map work, but sustained inquiry into the lives of people far and near. Further, many parents feel that real-life, nonacademic exposure to other cultures and positive parental models are the best remedy for insularity or provincialism. Living peaceably alongside our neighbors may be a multicultural education in itself.

If by "multicultural," then, we mean an interest in and appreciation of the variety of contemporary and historical human experience, then classical education fits the bill. In fact, by including historical as well as geographic and cultural diversity in our program of study, we help avoid a particularly prevalent form of modern bigotry: the chronological. As Cicero observed, "Whoever is ignorant of the past remains forever a child." Contemporary education methods, with their relentless innovations, promote the assumption that we have nothing to learn from the past.

Classical education remedies this ill by reminding us that the United States is hardly the first experiment in multiethnic living. As early as Herodotus, we see a healthy curiosity about and respect for other peoples and their practices. We have seen that the Roman Empire successfully faced the challenge of uniting a widely varied populace without imposing a stifling uniformity. Historical centers of classical learning existed not only in southern Europe, but also in the great Hellenistic cities of Africa, in the lonely Irish monastic outposts of the North Atlantic, and in the Muslim-ruled cities of medieval Spain. Some of the classical tradition's brightest lights came from far-flung corners of the Roman Empire; some, like Aesop or Epictetus, were slaves.

By grounding ourselves firmly in our own Western cultural milieu, we have a solid and reliable vantage point from which to evaluate and appreciate other cultures, past and present. We are freed from our cultural and chronological myopia and can afford to take long and broad views.

If, however, by "multicultural" is meant a political agenda based on cultural relativism and promoting a worldview that divides us all into victimizers and victimized—as the contemporary academic triumvirate of Race, Class, and Gender Studies would have it—then classical education is again guilty as charged. Classical education stands against the notion that all cultures and cultural practices are equally valid "in their own way" and most especially against the doctrine that right and wrong vary from place to place and across time. Rather, it calls upon its devotees to exercise discernment—formed and informed by constant exposure to the best—in judging any culture and its works. Classical education "is not so much uni-cultural as aristo-cultural—" writes Simmons, "it directs us to models of the best in all fields of human achievement."[78] In doing so, it allows us to take a sober look at all cultures, our own included, and to see clearly which have had the most enduring influence on the most people. It urges us to live up to our highest standards and to acknowledge, in all humility, the many times we have failed to do so.

Finally, classical education gives us a basis on which to judge the value of current trends and fashions. Will this novelist or that songwriter be remembered a hundred, two hundred, a thousand years

---

78 Simmons, p. 232.

from now? Classically educated people not only have a window into the past, but a clear view of today—and a vision of tomorrow.

III. *MULTUM NON MULTA:*
THE APPLICATION OF
AN EDUCATIONAL PRINCIPLE

We should not allow the good things to crowd out the best things.

—**Valerie Bendt**

ॐ

It is all well and good to look at historical curricula, but how do we put traditional classical education into practice today? Don't we have far more history to learn, not to mention science, modern languages, and common school subjects like health and driver's ed.? After all, we're not preparing our children to be Greek philosophers, Roman orators, or (most of us) British statesmen. We have practical matters to consider: government requirements, standardized tests, college admissions.

Yes, all that is true, at least to a certain extent. But we can still derive some important principles from the history of classical education.

As you look through the curriculum suggestions in the second part of this book, you will notice one of those principles at work. As articulated by Pliny the Younger, that principle is *multum non multa*: not many things (*multa*), but much (*multum*). The Greek version of this maxim—οὐ πολλ᾽ ἀλλὰ πολυ—conveys the same thought. Formal education should not merely introduce us to many things—the "multa," which can by necessity lead only to superficial knowledge—but should encourage us to drink deeply at the springs of our culture.

How does this play out in the classical curriculum?

First, the number of subjects is limited to a few key disciplines. We are accustomed to schools expanding their offerings to include vocational and technical subjects such a home economics, wood shop, and computer keyboarding. In the wry words of Jacques Barzun, we expect our schools to turn out "ideal citizens, supertolerant neighbors, agents of world peace, and happy family folk, at once sexually adept and flawless drivers of cars."[79] The classical curriculum insists on a limited number of demanding subjects taught in depth. Moreover, formal study of certain subjects—especially science and modern languages—is reserved for high school. As we'll see, this is actually an efficient use of the student's time and effort.

Second, whenever possible, subjects are taught in relation to one another and in the context of broader intellectual concerns. For example, as the student gains proficiency in Latin translation, some historical, literary, and theological readings may be undertaken in the original language. The student doesn't just read a chapter about Julius Caesar or Cicero in a history textbook; she reads Caesar's and Cicero's own writings in Latin. The study of selections from Thomas Aquinas's *Summa Theologica* is at once a lesson in Latin, logic, history, and theology.[80] Further, one of the key "intelligences" is lateral thinking, the ability to make connections between seemingly disparate fields and ideas, and the classical curriculum encourages this skill. Subjects like math and science, often treated apart from "arts and letters," are reintegrated into the humanities curriculum through biography, history, and ethics. In all subjects, students should be led to ask big questions: What is Man? What is the good life? How then should we live?

Third, the core readings in English and History (Classical Studies, Christian Studies, and Modern Studies) consist of a very few representative masterpieces that the student reads slowly and studies in depth. Does such a pared-down program sufficiently prepare students for college work, let alone life?

The verdict of history is yes. The great Renaissance educator Vittorio da Feltre assigned only four authors to his young students: Virgil, Homer, Cicero, and Demosthenes.[81] (These were, of course, read in the original Latin and Greek.) The traditional classical model emphasizes

---

79. Quoted in Simmons, p. 10.
80. See Martin Cothran, "Latin, Logic, and Christian Theology," http://www.memoriapress.com/articles/summa.html .
81. Hicks, p. 133.

the slow, careful reading of a small corpus of great literature—especially
the epic poets. Contrast this with the typical approach of contemporary
American schools:

> One cannot help but observe the trend in modern schools to sub-
> stitute light "escape" reading for the more difficult classics. The
> practice is defended in the name of getting students to read. The
> assumption is that because students learn to read by reading,
> schools must provide books that students will want to read, books
> that will not overtax their patience, their limited vocabulary, or
> even their more limited intelligence. A corollary to this assump-
> tion, as we have seen, is that students cannot enjoy reading serious
> classics with their demanding styles and remote contents. Clearly,
> the classical academy rejects this thesis. Not only does it refute the
> notion that classics are inaccessible or unenjoyable to young read-
> ers, but it reminds us that the purpose of learning is discovery, not
> escape. [...] Substituting the literature of escape for the classics is
> not education, but an attack on learning; it is not intellectual, but
> anti-intellectual. It represents a capitulation to the adolescent ap-
> petites of our students and our race.[82]

Tracy Lee Simmons minces no words on this subject:

> Most public schools in America now strive to be cut-rate educa-
> tional malls for the intellectually lame—whether or not students
> first darken the school doors that way, so most of them leave—
> while even some private schools pose as little more than colorful
> felt boards for the earnestly shallow, commonly confusing pious
> or patriotic piffle with real education.[83]

---

82. Hicks, p. 137.
83. Simmons, p. 186.

Unfortunately, this trend is noticeable even among home schoolers. Popular neoclassical programs suggest that students in the early grades read many children's novels—slight, if entertaining, books hardly worthy of the sustained attention given them in the English curriculum. While truly "good books" are an excellent and necessary preparation for the Great Books,[84] they may most profitably be read independently or within the family circle, not as part of formal schooling. Later, students are rushed through the whole Western canon in a few years of Great Books, with reading lists based on those of university programs. For example, the formal reading list for the seventh grade presented in one popular guide includes a dizzying twenty-one books, ranging from *Don Quixote* (an abridged version is permitted) to *Pilgrim's Progress* to the Grimms' fairy tales to *Pride and Prejudice*. And this is only for English! Another publisher's recommendations for the same year include eighteen titles, taking the student through Genesis in a week and the whole of the Iliad in five. At the same time, the students are also reading a work of theology, a study on ancient cities, the *Epic of Gilgamesh*, and a challenging adult novel by C. S. Lewis. Even with wonderful, meaty selections like these, one has to wonder how much young teens are really getting out of plowing through the Great Books at such a break-neck pace.

By contrast, Simmons reminds us that "[s]chools of the best kind have always aimed high while keeping feet to the ground. They didn't try to do too much; they tried to do the most important things."[85]

The core readings suggested here focus on those "important things"—the few truly enduring and representative literary monuments of the past 2,500 years. Ample time is given for students to read, re-read, and "live into" their schoolbooks. As will be seen in the following discussion, the ancients possessed an effective method for approaching their great classics—which were no easier for the schoolboys of A.D. 100 than they are for our daughters and sons. The difference is that the grammar-

---

84. Cf. Dr. James Taylor, "From Good to Great," talk given at the 2003 CiRCE Conference.
85. Simmons, p. 186.

ians and rhetors were highly selective in the texts they placed before their students. These works were models both of style and of their culture's aesthetic and moral norms. We would do well to take seriously their approach.

Does this mean that students will go through thirteen years of schooling never cracking an English novel? Are we denying our children the pleasure of floating down the river with Rat and Mole, bursting with excitement when Almanzo wins first prize for his milk-fed pumpkin, or pushing past a row of old coats to step into the Narnian winter? Of course not. What it does mean is that we apply the principle of *multum non multa* in selecting schoolbooks. The streamlined classical curriculum leaves plenty of free time for other pursuits, including reading for pleasure and discovery. It is in these free hours that students can sail the seas to *Treasure Island*, sit in the drawing rooms of Austen and Trollope, thrill to the daring escapades of *The Scarlet Pimpernel*, march with the Roman legions in *Eagle of the Ninth*, circle the globe with Phileas Fogg, or experience the angst of modern dystopias in *1984* and *Brave New World*.

In addition to studying the core readings in depth, then, the student is expected to read independently every day, and families are strongly encouraged to read aloud for at least one hour three times a week. Daily is better. If time does not permit parents and children to read together regularly, high-quality audio books and dramatizations may prove helpful. Independent and family reading is linked to schoolwork and enriches it, but should not be considered part of the formal school day. Rather, this time introduces the student to a wide range of English literature and foreign works in translation, establishes the habit of daily reading, and draws families together.

The advantages of the *multum non multa* approach are many. Eliminating busywork—workbooks, redundant curricula, excessive "escape" reading—from the school day cuts the student's work time tremendously. Rolling subjects together—Latin and logic, Greek and geometry, history and literature—further reduces wasted time and mental energy. The time savings may be applied to the student's own interests and to enrichment subjects such as sports, dance, or cooking. Parents will find that their preparation time is much reduced as they eliminate redundant subjects and learn alongside their children. Parents may also enjoy considerable savings on formal curricula, perhaps freeing funds for music lessons, building a quality home library, or other family needs.

Let us now look at how the principle of *multum non multa* is applied across the curriculum. In the following discussion, special emphasis is given to the areas that differ the most from the neoclassical model and other more familiar approaches.

The Mother Tongue:
Multum non Multa *and Language Mastery*

What distinguishes the traditional classical curriculum from other approaches is the central position of the classical languages, especially Latin. It is from this focus that the terms "Latin-based" or "Latin-centered" come. These terms are perhaps unfortunate, since they sometimes mislead people into thinking that the classical curriculum teaches Latin to the complete exclusion of other important subjects, like English. While this may have been the case a few centuries ago, it is not what I am suggesting here. It is, however, true that by making Latin the focus of the home school reduces the time spent on "language arts" work in English.

We have already touched on some of the ways the *multum non multa* principle affects curriculum choices in English, e.g., by reducing the number of core books. Here are some other ways that focusing on Latin can streamline your English curriculum:

1. *A strong Latin course virtually eliminates the need for a separate vocabulary program,* since the bulk of the most difficult English vocabulary is Latinate. As Cheryl Lowe points out, any child who knows that the simple Latin word pater means "father" will have no problems figuring out the meaning of words like "patriarch, patriarchy, paternal, paternalistic, patron, patronize, paternity, patrimony."[86] Likewise, Latin reduces the need for a formal spelling curriculum; spelling can be taught through copywork and individualized drill on an as-needed basis.

2. *The study of Latin grammar reduces or even eliminates the need for a formal English grammar program in the elementary years.*[87] This idea has met with much incredulity among neoclassical home schoolers, yet we need only look at the literary products of past centuries to see that Latin provides all the English grammar practice anyone needs, and more. Consider the following assessment:

> The absence of English instruction from English education at this time [the seventeenth century], though, should not send us down the wrong road. English was given its due in the ebullient stage of its life; the quality of English poetry and prose penned in this age should leave no doubt that this was a great age of English style. But the brightest minds thought that mastery with English—or at least mastery with English of the best kind came by way of classical training.[88]

Those who remain skeptical will be happy to know that most modern Latin programs, including those recommended here, introduce or review basic English grammar. Likewise, one of the popular composition programs, *Classical Writing*, integrates the formal study of English grammar.

86. Cheryl Lowe, "Latin Is the Next Step after Phonics," *The Classical Teacher*, Summer 2004, p. 20.

87. Cheryl Lowe addresses this issue in her excellent 2003 CiRCE Conference talk, "Latin: What It Does for the Student and the School."

88. Simmons, p. 123.

3. *Latin translation and composition provide excellent training in English composition.* Here is Simmons again:

> Writing in Latin especially spurs us to speak and write in complete sentences containing complete thoughts: a complete sentence *is* a complete thought. [...] Latin composition encourages us to structure the things we have to say before we say them. It teaches us to communicate efficiently and well with finely tuned clauses and well-considered words. The practice of Latin composition helps to eradicate loose thinking and feeling. [...] Practice with Latin composition tightens expression. We learn to be brief.[89]

What is left, then, of English? As described here, English Studies parallels the Greco-Roman grammar and rhetoric courses described by Quintilian and others. It includes two branches: literature and composition. I recommend the careful reading of a small number of acknowledged masterpieces; abundant independent and family reading; copywork as a medium for instruction in spelling and usage; a brief overview of English grammar in eighth grade; and a formal progression of rhetorical studies in English, beginning with the *progymnasmata* (elementary composition exercises), continuing through a reading of Aristotle's *Rhetoric*, and culminating in several in-depth research papers by the end of high school.

The Classical Heritage:
Multum non Multa *and Historical Studies*

The definition of classical education that I proposed in the first chapter of this book does not limit us to the study of classical languages. It includes classical cultures—their history, literature, and art—as well.

---

89. Simmons, p. 170.

The study of history in the United States has long languished, and we read not only of the ignorance of our high school and college graduates, but even of our nation's leaders. One of the great appeals of neoclassical education is its strong emphasis on chronological history. *The Well-Trained Mind*, for example, takes the student through world history in three four-year cycles. Veritas Press also recommends three cycles, but stretches the first out over five years (second to sixth grade) before integrating history with literature in its Omnibus (Great Books) course.

Other classical-style programs divide history into two streams, studying world history and national history simultaneously. This is the method of the acclaimed Core Knowledge Sequence, championed by E. D. Hirsch, Jr., and of some Charlotte Mason-influenced home school programs, such as Ambleside Online. This dual approach is also common in tradition-minded European schools.

There are advantages and disadvantages to both methods. The strict chronological approach, working from whole to parts, gives students the big picture first and fills in the details later. It places national history—particularly that of comparatively young nations like the United States, Canada, and Australia—in the wider context of world history. It successfully conveys the overall flow of history, allowing students to see parallels between different civilizations, such as the fact that ancient cultures tended to grow up and flourish alongside rivers, or that medieval Europe and Japan developed analogous feudal societies. Contemporary elementary history books, like Susan Wise Bauer's excellent four-volume *Story of the World*, generally do a good job of including non-Western cultures.

But some parents are concerned that following the strict chronological approach means that their students will have no formal study of national history until third grade, and that such study is then condensed into only a year and a half. Likewise, it is difficult to obtain more than a cursory familiarity with the people and cultures of the ancient world in a single year; by necessity, some key figures will be overlooked.

(For example, one popular introduction to the ancients never mentions Socrates.) While this is perhaps understandable in a text meant for the early elementary years, the rapidity of the four-year cycle makes it very difficult for students at any level to gain familiarity with the cultures that have most influenced our own.

A multi-stream approach to history encourages elementary students to move at a slower pace, lingering over complex issues and gaining intimate knowledge of people, movements, and ideas. It gives more detailed exposure to national history, and from an earlier age. Moreover, it allows ample time for the study of the Greek and Roman cultures, which we have seen is central to classical education.

The primary concern voiced about this method is that students will not understand the broad sweep of history, but a simple timeline is all that is needed to help younger students grasp the concept of linear history. High school students undertake a broader study of world history trends at a time when they are better able to make connections between what they are learning in world history and their knowledge in other fields—science, art, and ethics or theology. This method moves from parts to whole, from the concrete and detailed to the abstract and overarching. If we accept Dorothy Sayers' assessment of the child's intellectual development, we will see that this slower, parts-to-whole approach fits it perhaps even better than the strict chronological approach.

How does the multi-stream approach to history work? In the schedules and curriculum charts later in this book, you will find several subjects that correspond to history and geography or "social studies." Note that these subjects also incorporate a great deal of literature. The first is Classical Studies, which covers the geography, history, and literature of the ancient Greece and Rome. Christian Studies explores ancient history from a Biblical perspective; covers the Dark Ages, Middle Ages, and Reformation; and includes selected works by twentieth-century Christian writers. (Some literature of these periods is covered in English

Studies.) Modern Studies[90] covers history from the early modern period and continues to the present, with a focus on national history. Again, some of the literature selections in English Studies correspond to this period. Details of each of these subjects will be found in the curriculum chapters that follow. Both rely on the same method that we've already seen applied to English: a core of excellent masterworks, studied slowly and in-depth, and integrated into the rest of the curriculum.

Multum non Multa *and the Quadrivium*

A detailed discussion of other subjects will be found below. At this point, we can take a quick look at how the principle of *multum non multa* plays out in science and mathematics.

Science

Because it requires a high level of abstract thinking, science is best studied informally before high school. In the early years, the focus is on concrete facts: the processes of the natural world, from the social structure of the beehive to the orbits of the planets. Students read books from the public library or their own collections and observe nature first-hand. In eighth grade they study a book aimed at encouraging scientific literacy, preparing them for in-depth study of the sciences in high school. At all levels, the history of science and ethical concerns play a central role in the science curriculum, and students are encouraged to bring the fundamental questions of classical thought—What is Man? What is the good life?—to bear on scientific inquiry.

---

90. This subject combines modern world history with national history, so can be adapted for readers in any country. An example of the multi-stream approach can be seen in the Highlands Latin School (www.thelatinschool.com), from which I have borrowed some of the names of these subjects.

Arithmetic and Mathematics

Mathematics, along with Latin, is at the center of the classical curriculum. After all, next to the Trivium's language arts stands the Quadrivium—the mathematical arts. Students gain basic numeracy through slow and steady mastery of arithmetic facts in the early grades, gradually building toward the formal study of algebra and Euclidean geometry in high school. As with science, math studies include history and biography, linking this subject to the broader history of thought and to ethics.

IV. SCOPE AND SEQUENCE OVERVIEW AND SAMPLE SCHEDULES

ℰ✺

Primary School

	Kindergarten	Grade 1	Grade 2
English Studies	Intensive phonics; Nursery rhymes and nursery tales; Copywork; Recitation	Intensive phonics; fairy tales, *50 Famous Stories Retold*; Copywork; Recitation	Phonics as needed; *50 Famous Stories Retold,* tall tales, folk legends; Copywork; Recitation
Latin	Prima Latina Vocabulary & Sayings	Prima Latina	Latina Christiana I, Ludere Latine
Classical Studies	Aesop's Fables	Greek and Roman myths (picture books)	Norse myths
Christian Studies	Bible stories, memory verses, prayers, catechism	Bible stories, memory verses, prayers, catechism	Bible stories, memory verses, prayers, catechism
Modern Studies	Geography topics; biographies	Geography topics; biographies	Geography topics; biographies
Arithmetic		Rod & Staff, Ray's Arithmetic, or curriculum of choice	Rod & Staff, Ray's Arithmetic, or curriculum of choice
Nature Study (Science)	Informal nature study	Informal nature study	Informal nature study

Note: During the primary-school years, aim for at least one hour of daily family reading. You may include the reading for English Studies, Classical Studies, and Christian Studies in this total.

Early Grammar School

	3	4	5
English Studies (includes Progymnasmata)	Hawthorne's *Wonder Book, Tanglewood Tales*; Progymnasmata: Fable; Copywork; Recitation	Lambs' *Tales from Shakespeare*; Progymnasmata: Narrative; Copywork; Recitation	Roger Lancelyn Green's *King Arthur and His Knights of the Round Table*; Tolkien's *The Hobbit*; Shakespeare, "A Midsummer Night's Dream"; Progymnasmata: Chreia, Maxim; Copywork, Recitation
Latin	Latina Christiana I/II, Ludere Latine	Latina Christiana II, Ludere Latine	Henle I (Units 1-2)
Greek	Elementary Greek I	Elementary Greek I	Elementary Greek II
Classical Studies	D'Aulaires' *Greek Myths*	*Famous Men of Rome*	*The Boys' and Girls' Plutarch** or *Famous Men of Greece*
Christian Studies	Christian Studies I	Christian Studies II	Christian Studies III
Modern Studies	Artner Units 1 & 2 Geography topics	Artner 3 Geography topics	Artner 4 Geography topics
Arithmetic	Rod & Staff, Ray's, or curriculum of choice	Rod & Staff, Ray's, or curriculum of choice	Rod & Staff, Ray's, or curriculum of choice
Nature Study	Informal nature study	Informal nature study	Informal nature study

* ed. John S. White; online at digital.library.upenn.edu/webbin/gutbook/lookup?num=2484

Note: In third grade, students should be reading independently for a minimum of 30 minutes a day, increasing to one hour by fifth grade. Additional family read-alouds of one hour a day should be the rule whenever possible.

Late Grammar School

	6	7	8
English Studies (includes Progymnasmata)	Progymnasmata: Refutation, Confirmation; Common Topic; Copywork; Recitation *For this year's literature selections, see Classical Studies	"Julius Caesar"*; Progymnasmata: Encomium, Invective, Comparison; Copywork; Recitation *For primary literature selection, see Classical Studies	*Lord of the Rings*; Progymnasmata: Characterization and Description, Thesis, Law; *Our Mother Tongue, The Elements of Style;* Copywork; Recitation
Latin	Henle I (Units 3-5)	Henle I (Units 6-10), (see also Christian Studies)	Henle I (Units 11-14); *Esopus Hodie, Fabulae Graecae,* (see also Christian Studies)
Greek	Elementary Greek II	Elementary Greek III	Elementary Greek III
Logic		Traditional Logic I	Traditional Logic II
Classical Studies	Homer: *Iliad* and *Odyssey*	Virgil: *The Aeneid*	Aeschylus: *The Oresteia*
Christian Studies	Lingua Angelica	Lingua Angelica	*The Abolition of Man, Mere Christianity,* Lingua Biblica
Modern Studies	Artner 5 Geography topics	Artner 6 Geography topics	Artner 7 & 8; Geography topics; *Roots of American Order*
Arithmetic	Rod & Staff, Ray's, or curriculum of choice	Rod & Staff, Ray's, or curriculum of choice	Rod & Staff, Ray's, or curriculum of choice
Science	Informal nature study	Informal nature study	*Science Matters*

Note: Remember to include one hour each of independent and family reading every day.

Secondary School

	9	10	11	12
English Studies (includes Rhetoric)	*Beowulf, Sir Gawain and the Green Knight, Canterbury Tales* (selections); Rhetoric with Aristotle; Recitation	*Divine Comedy*; Recitation	Shakespeare; Recitation	English Poets; Recitation
Latin	Henle II (Caesar), Lessons 1-20	Henle II, Lessons 21-32	Henle III (Cicero)	Henle IV (Virgil), or AP Catullus for advanced students
Greek	Attic or Koine text	Attic or Koine text; selected readings	*Anabasis* (Book I)	Homer (selections)
Logic	Material Logic I	Material Logic II (forthcoming) or Logical Fallacies	Plato's *Dialogues* and Kreeft's *Socratic Logic* (optional)	Plato's *Dialogues* and Kreeft's *Socratic Logic* (optional)
Classical Studies	Sophocles: Theban plays, Euripides: *The Bacchantes*; Aristotle: *Poetics*	Aristotle: *Nicomachean Ethics*	Marcus Aurelius: *Meditations*	Plato: *The Republic*
Christian Studies	Job	Isaiah	Gospel of John (portions in Greek)	Epistle to the Romans; *Pilgrim's Progress*
Modern Studies	Churchill, vol. 1	Churchill, vol. 2	Churchill, vol. 3	Churchill, vol. 4
Mathematics	Geometry (Euclid)	Algebra I	Algebra II	Optional: Pre-Calculus
Science	Earth Science or General Science I	Biology or General Science II	Optional: Chemistry	Optional: Physics

Note: Independent and family reading should continue as in late grammar school.

About Scheduling

Every family must approach the question of scheduling from its own unique perspective. A family home schooling one child will have a very different schedule from the family of five who are close in age, and the schedule will be very different again if the home school consists of a high schooler and a kindergartner. Single-parent families will schedule differently from families in which one or both parents are at home. Children growing up on a working farm will have different family responsibilities from children growing up in a city. Further, the amount of time it will take any individual child to complete a day's work is difficult to predict, and will change with the curriculum, the child's temperament, and age. Therefore, the schedules here should be taken as mere suggestions only.

A few general principles do apply. Classical languages (Latin and Greek) and math should be given the bulk of the student's time and his best hours, whenever those may be. Time should also be allotted daily for copywork; recitation and memory work in the various subjects; music practice; and independent and family reading. These are your "must-do" subjects. The other subjects—English Studies (including the *progymnasmata* and Rhetoric), Classical Studies, Christian Studies, Modern Studies, Nature Study/Science, and Logic—should be scheduled on a weekly or semi-weekly rotation.

The arrangement of the schedule will change as your student moves through the curriculum. A primary-age child will typically need short blocks of time and more variation than a grammar-age child, and a secondary-school student will benefit from studying fewer subjects in a day but for substantial chunks of time. In all cases, do make allowances for individual needs. Some students can buckle down nicely for an hour or more of Latin; others will need frequent breaks. The suggested times are just that—suggestions. You will determine, through trial and error, what works best for your student in a given season of her life.

Sample Primary School Schedule

	Monday	Tuesday	Wednesday	Thursday	Friday
9:00-9:20	Latin	Latin	Latin	Latin	Latin
9:30-10:00	Arithmetic	Arithmetic	Arithmetic	Arithmetic	Arithmetic
10:00-10:20	Music Practice	Music Practice	Music Practice	Music Practice	Music Practice
10:45-11:00	Copywork and Recitation	Copywork and Recitation	Copywork and Recitation	Copywork and Recitation	Copywork and Recitation
11:00-11:30	Phonics	Phonics	Phonics	Phonics	Phonics
11:30-12:30	Lunch and Playtime	Lunch and Playtime	Lunch and Playtime	Lunch and Playtime	Lunch and Playtime
12:30-1:00	English Studies*	Christian Studies*	Modern Studies*	Nature Study	Classical Studies*

* In the Primary School, these subjects will consist primarily of read-alouds.

Sample Grammar School Schedule

	Monday	Tuesday	Wednesday	Thursday	Friday
9:00-9.45	Latin	Latin	Latin	Latin	Latin
9:45-10:00	Copywork and Recitation	Copywork and Recitation	Copywork and Recitation	Copywork and Recitation	Copywork and Recitation
10:00-11:00	Arithmetic	Arithmetic	Arithmetic	Arithmetic	Arithmetic
11:00-11:30	Music Practice	Music Practice	Music Practice	Music Practice	Music Practice
11:30-12:15	Greek	Greek	Greek	Greek	Greek
12:15-1:00	Lunch	Lunch	Lunch	Lunch	Lunch
1:00-2:00	English Studies: Progym	English Studies: Literature	English Studies: Progym	English Studies: Literature	English Studies: Progym
2:00-3:00	Classical Studies	Christian Studies	Modern Studies	Nature Study	

Note: In creating your own schedule, do include short breaks between subjects and try to break up "seat work" with other activities, like music practice.

Sample Secondary School Schedule

	Monday	Tuesday	Wednesday	Thursday	Friday
8:00-9:30	Math	Greek	Math	Greek	Math
10:00-11:30	Latin	Logic	Latin	Science	Latin
11:30-12:15	Lunch	Lunch	Lunch	Lunch	Lunch
12:15-1:00	Music Practice	Music Practice	Music Practice	Music Practice	Music Practice
1:00-3:00	English Studies	Classical Studies	Rhetoric	Christian Studies	Modern Studies

V. CLASSICAL LANGUAGES: LATIN AND GREEK

Not to know Greek is to be ignorant of the most flexible and subtle instrument of expression that the human mind has devised, and not to know Latin is to have missed an admirable training in precise and logical thought.

—Sir Richard Livingstone

ℰↃ

Latin and Greek are the subjects that put the *classical* in "classical education." I recommend an early start in Latin, but this should not be taken as an all-or-nothing imperative; some students may benefit from waiting until third or even fifth grade to begin Latin. If you are beginning a classical curriculum with an older student, start from where you are.

Latin is one of your daily, must-do subjects; remember, in the classical curriculum, Latin is the spine of your whole language arts program.

Greek may be added two or more years after beginning Latin or delayed until secondary school. If begun in the grammar-school years, Greek should also be studied daily. If you delay Greek until later, you may opt for several large blocks of study time rather than shorter daily periods.

Latin

First, a note on that perennial topic of debate: Latin pronunciation. The curricula I recommend use ecclesiastical (church) pronunciation ("vayni, veedee, veechee"). There are a number of reasons to prefer this to either the reconstructed classical pronunciation ("wenee, weedee, weekee") or the older "English" pronunciation ("veni, vidi, vissi"). First, it is the pronunciation we are used to hearing in Western classical music, which is all the Latin most of us are likely to encounter on a regular basis. It is, as the name indicates, the language of the Western church, and as such has a venerable history that continues in this day. It was the pronunciation known to Dante and other medieval writers. Ecclesiastical pronunciation is similar to modern Italian, making it easier to learn that language if one so chooses. Finally, it is simply beautiful to hear, to speak, and to sing. At base, however, the choice of pronunciation is personal, and there are any number of reasons that a family might wish to use the classical pronunciation—a parent's or student's previous experience, for example, or the availability of a co-op class that uses it. Whatever you decide, rest assured that no native Latin speakers are going to pop up to correct you![91]

Curriculum Overview

	Primary School	Grammar School	Secondary School
Goals	Gentle introduction to Latin pronunciation and vocabulary	Memorize the Latin grammar; begin reading and translation of Latin literature	Read and translate Latin literature; prepare for AP exams (optional)
Materials	Prima Latina, Lingua Angelica CD, "I Am Reading Latin" series	Latina Christiana I and II; Lingua Angelica I and II; Lingua Biblica; Henle Latin I	Henle Latin II-IV, additional readings

---

91. For a discussion of the advantages of Christian Latin, see Dorothy Sayers' essay, "The Single Greatest Defect of My Latin Education," available online at www.memoriapress.com/articles/sayers-intropage.html .

Latin in the Primary-School Years (K-2)

During the primary years, give your students a gentle introduction to Latin that emphasizes vocabulary words, phrases, and prayers. Plan to spend no more than 15-20 minutes a day on Latin at this stage.

Kindergarten - Second Grade

In the Primary grades, children begin their exposure to Latin with **Prima Latina** (Memoria Press). This very gentle text introduces simple vocabulary and prayers, as well as the parts of speech. It also provides a solid English grammar foundation so students are prepared for future Latin study. Although some classical educators feel that students should not begin Latin until they are reading well, this program has been used successfully with pre-readers, by having the students complete the exercises orally. This is a good approach for a younger sibling who wants to "do school" with the older children but is not ready to read the text independently. Pronunciation CDs and instructional DVDs are also available. The program is very easy to use, even for parents with no previous Latin background.

If you are looking for some variety for your young students, you can include a few supplements. The **I Am Reading Latin** series from Bolchazy-Carducci Publishers (www.bolchazy.com) consists of four simple picture books with words for animals, numbers, family members, colors, and food in Latin. A read-along CD is available, but it uses classical pronunciation; if you are using Memoria Press's materials, you may want to skip the CD to avoid confusing your students and just read the books aloud using the ecclesiastical pronunciation you've learned in *Prima Latina*. **Minimus**, a classroom text for elementary students, offers another enrichment possibility. It presents a historic Roman family living in Britain and uses the direct method—spoken Latin through dialogues. Skip the grammar and just enjoy the dialogues, historical background, and myths. The second volume of the series, *Minimus Secundus*, continues the story with more complex vocabulary and grammar forms. Finally, you can easily integrate music into your Latin studies with Memoria Press's excellent **Lingua Angelica**. At this stage you need only the CD and, for your own reference, the lyric book; the other parts of the program focus on translation skills and will be used in the later grammar years. Young students are particularly fond of the beautiful Gregorian chant. Consider playing *Lingua Angelica* during rest time or as background music to seat work.

After you have completed *Prima Latina*, move along in the Memoria Press curriculum sequence to **Latina Christiana I.** Flash cards, instructional DVDs, and grammar charts are available, and the book also contains historical information keyed to *Famous Men of Rome*. (Your student will be studying this book in depth in fourth grade, so there is no need to study it in detail now.)

Since you are beginning early with this text, take it as slowly as necessary. The suggested schedule allows you a year and a half to finish the book, so there is no need to rush. When you finish the first book, begin **Latina Christiana II**. If your student's work is solid, move forward at an accelerated pace. If you find your student is floundering, move more slowly. Some parents may find that they need to delay formal Latin study for another year or two. You can begin with *Latina Christiana* as late as fourth or fifth grade and still finish memorizing the Latin grammar before high school. Just continue reviewing *Prima Latina*, listening to *Lingua Angelica*, and enjoying the *I Am Reading Latin* books until your student is ready for *Latina Christiana*.

Latin in the Grammar-School Years (3-8)

The prime directive in the grammar-school years is to memorize the Latin grammar. This is the foundation of all further work in Latin and, one could argue, of the classical curriculum itself. Give Latin your student's best hour of the day, perhaps first thing in the morning while he's still fresh. Plan to spend 30-45 minutes a day in the early grammar years, working up to an hour as the student approaches high school.

Third Grade

Continue (or begin) **Latina Christiana II**. Do not be afraid to move slowly through this material, particularly since this year sees the introduction of some more challenging reading in other subjects. Make sure the student knows the forms and vocabulary cold before you move on. You may need to take two years to cover all of *Latina Christiana II,* beginning Henle in fifth grade.

Fourth and Fifth Grades

When your student has mastered the contents of both volumes of *Latina Christiana,* it is time to move on to **Henle First Year**. The student may be ready in the fourth grade or in sixth. The important factor, however, is not the grade, but to achieve mastery before moving on to the next level.

Henle is a high school textbook, but do not be intimidated! Your child can do this, and so can you. Henle presents grammar systematically and with a minimum of vocabulary, allowing the necessary time to master the forms. Plan to complete Units 1-2, which present the five noun declensions and adjectives, in fifth grade. The forms in Unit 1 will be review, but the exercises are copious and require much care and increasing time. Memoria Press publishes two helpful guides to Henle, written by Cheryl Lowe. The first covers units 1 and 2; the second, units 3 through 5. Feel free to modify the pace as needed. Another study alternative is the HenleLatin list at Yahoo!Groups. This online study group, run by a dedicated classical home schooling mom, allow students to work through the Henle texts at their own pace via private email lists. Visit groups.yahoo.com/group/HenleLatin for more information.

Sixth Grade

In sixth grade, plan to complete Units 3-5, which cover all four conjugations in six tenses, active and passive; and personal pronouns.

Seventh Grade

This year's study consists of **Henle First Year,** units 6-10. Again, set the pace according to your student's abilities, striving for mastery of all grammar forms and vocabulary before moving on. For translation, you will be using Memoria Press's **Lingua Angelica** program; see the seventh-grade section of Christian Studies for more details. You may not translate all of the hymns in *Lingua Angelica* in one year, but it still serves as a great introduction to Latin translation.

Eighth Grade

This year your student completes **Henle First Year**, units 11-14, and begins independent translation work.

For additional translation you may stay with *Lingua Angelica* or move to **Lingua Biblica** to translate passages from the Vulgate (Latin Bible). Alternatively, you can use familiar passages from the Vulgate (Latin Bible), available as **Fabulae Vulgatae** at www.mythfolklore.net/bible/stories.htm; **Esopus Hodie**, a beginning reader available from the American Classics League (www.aclclassics.org.tmrc) or the Latin edition of Aesop at www.mythfolklore.net/aesopica/; or selections from **Fabulae Graecae** (ISBN 0801307562). This last is also available online at www.mythfolklore.net/fabulaefaciles/index.htm .

Latin in the Secondary-School Years (9-12)

Plan to spend 60-90 minutes a day on Latin until the student has completed *Henle Second Year*. After that you can allot two or three 90-minute sessions a week to Latin.

Ninth Grade

In this transitional year, the ninth grader begins **Henle Second Year**, Lessons 1-20, which has the student reading Caesar's *Gallic Wars*. Plan to work through the first twenty lessons this year; the remainder of the book will be completed in the ninth grade. This is also a good time to introduce the classical pronunciation of Latin, if the student has not already encountered it.

Tenth Grade

Complete **Henle Second Year,** lessons 21-32. A few additional grammar points are introduced; this will be the last of the new grammar.

Eleventh Grade

Eleventh grade brings the student to **Henle Third Year** and readings from Cicero. No new grammar is introduced, but the student will find it interesting to read Cicero after having studied Aristotle in the ninth and tenth grades.

Twelfth Grade

In twelfth grade the student completes the Henle sequence with **Henle Fourth Year** and the reading of Virgil. As the content of the story will be familiar from the student's in-depth reading in seventh grade, the focus can turn to the work's poetic technique and literary themes.

Vergil's Aeneid by Clyde Pharr (ISBN 0865164339) is an alternative to Henle. It provides the Latin text with reader notes, vocabulary, grammar, etc. The student may prepare for the Advanced Placement-Virgil exam if desired.

Advanced Twelfth Grade

If your student was able to progress through the Latin series ahead of the prescribed schedule, continue practice in translation by reading selections from St. Augustine, the *Summa Theologica* of Thomas Aquinas, and from a medieval anthology such as Helen Waddell's *Book of Medieval Latin for Schools* (OOP but available through used book sellers). If you aren't able to locate a copy of Waddell, a nice selection of medieval texts for translation is available online at www.mythfolklore.net/medieval_latin/ . Alternatively, the student may prepare for the AP Catullus exam (a tutor may be useful) or enroll in an upper-level Latin translation course at a community college.

Texts for translation, including Augustine's *Confessions* and portions of the *Summa*, can be found online at the Corpus Scriptorum Latinorum site: www.forumromanum.org/literature/index.html .

> **For Parents:**
>
> Many resources for teaching Latin at all levels can be found at the Web site of the American Classical League (www.aclclassics.org/) and their bookstore (www.aclclassics.org/tmrc/)

Greek

Without a knowledge of Greek there is no education. —**Leo Tolstoy**

There are two possible approaches to studying Greek. One is to begin with *koine* (the Hellenistic Greek of the Bible), just as one began with ecclesiastical Latin. Study of *koine* can begin about two years after commencing formal Latin grammar studies with *Latina Christiana.* If you follow the sequence suggested here, this would be in third grade, although the student can begin learning the alphabet and pronunciation earlier. Of course, if you start Latin later, Greek will also be pushed back. Another option is to delay Greek until high school and begin either with a standard college-level Biblical Greek text or with a traditional Attic grammar text such as Crosby and Schaeffer's *Introduction to Greek,* depending on the student's interests. It is best to delay Greek study if the student is struggling with Latin in the grammar-school years.

There are certain advantages to starting with *koine*—the grammar is somewhat simpler, the key Bible texts tend to be familiar and therefore easier to translate, there are many study helps and reference works available—but for many home schoolers the deciding factor is the simple fact that there currently exists no elementary-school curriculum for Attic Greek. So *koine* it is. Happily, Open Texture has recently published the first volume of a new program, *Elementary Greek: Koine for Beginners* by Christine Gatchell (www.opentexture.com). The remaining volumes are expected before the end of the school year 2005-2006. *Elementary Greek* is based on J. Gresham Machen's standard Biblical Greek textbook, making the transition to higher-level studies easier. The program takes a solid, grammar-centered approach comparable to *Latina Christiana*'s, and includes memory material. An audio CD, using Erasmian pronunciation, rounds out the program.[92]

---

92. As is the case with Latin, Greek pronunciation is subject to a number of competing conventions. The Erasmian pronunciation, used in Gatchell's program, is the standard in seminaries and many American academic settings. An alternative, comparable to the ecclesiastical pronunciation

Most parents will find it necessary to learn Greek alongside their children. This is certainly possible with any of the available Greek curricula and also with upper-level Biblical Greek texts; you may find learning Attic on your own more daunting. Unless you have significant background in classical Greek, I recommend that you consider a tutor, co-op class, or a community college for Attic. If your student is sticking with Biblical Greek, a local seminary may allow a motivated student to enroll in their language classes or can at least provide contact with tutors.

Greek in the Grammar-School Years (3-8)

Third-Eighth Grades

Begin with **Elementary Greek** two or more years after beginning Latin. This course has three levels, and the suggested schedule takes a gentle pace, allowing two years for each level. Students with solid language skills and those who begin the program after third grade will be able to move more quickly through the levels, in which case they may wish to devote the remainder of the grammar-school years to an adult-level textbook, such as Machen's *New Testament Greek for Beginners* (a workbook is available) or Mounce's *Basics of Biblical Greek Grammar.* A workbook, flash cards, vocabulary CD, and graded reader are available to supplement Mounce's text; the reader (ISBN 0310205824) may be used with any program.

Use the same learning techniques for Greek as for Latin: go slowly, overlearn the forms, leave long vocabulary lists for later. Do pay special attention to the rules of accentuation, which are rather more complex in Greek than in Latin. Greek study will require perhaps 30 minutes a day at this level.

---

in Latin, is the Byzantine or "ethnic" pronunciation, which is similar to modern Greek and is the norm in the Eastern Orthodox world. For more details on *koine* pronunciation options, see www.biblicalgreek.org/links/pronunciation.html .

You will want to have on hand a simple Greek grammar such William G. MacDonald's inexpensive *Greek Enchiridion: A Concise Handbook of Grammar for Translation and Exegesis* (ISBN 0913573183) and a compact lexicon (dictionary). The standard lexicons for scholars are very expensive; a smaller student edition such a G. Abbott-Smith's *Manual Greek Lexicon of the New Testament* (ISBN 0567086844) will be sufficient at this stage.

As your student progresses through the Greek grammar, you may want to supplement his study with some additional practice in translation. Aesop's *Fables*, the venerable first translation text favored by Erasmus, can be found in Greek online at www.mythfolklore.net/aesopica/. (English and Latin versions are also available at the same site.) The Greek gospels, divided into daily segments, are at www.mythfolklore. net/gospel/daily/index.htm . Finally, the Septuagint (Greek translation of the Old Testament) and the New Testament can be found at www. zhubert.com/ .

Greek in the Secondary-School Years (9-12)

Ninth and Tenth Grades

If your student is beginning with Biblical Greek, start either William Mounce's **Basics of Biblical Greek Grammar** (a workbook and other study materials are available) or J. Gresham Machen's **New Testament Greek for Beginners.** Students with previous experience in *koine* can start directly on Mounce's **Graded Reader of Biblical Greek** and then move to translating the New Testament. Additional online resources are listed in the "Greek in the Grammar-School Years" section.

Students with no prior Greek study who wish to begin Attic at this face a challenge. Unless the parent-teacher has a strong background in the language, I strongly suggest finding a tutor or class. While I do not want to discourage able students and their dedicated parents, the fact remains that classical Greek is not an easy language to learn on one's own, and there are few truly self-teaching curricula available. Some modern textbooks, such as the Cambridge *Reading Greek* course, can be used for independent study, but in my experience the success rate with these tends to be quite low without the guidance of an experienced teacher. Further, such courses do not emphasize the systematic study of grammar that is so vital if one wishes to master the language.

For students who have been studying *koine,* the transition should not be so difficult. Of the older traditional textbooks, I recommend Crosby and Schaeffer's **Introduction to Greek**, a standard secondary-school textbook from the early twentieth century, available in an affordable paperback edition from Bolchazy-Carducci (ISBN 0865165548). This is a traditional, no-frills text with copious English-to-Greek exercises, and it is very effective if the student is willing to work hard at it. Unfortunately, there is, as far as I know, no teacher's manual or answer key, so it is usable only by a teacher with substantial knowledge of the language. An even less expensive alternative is John Williams White's **First Greek Book**, available for free download from www.textkit.com . The TextKit site also sponsors study groups. Of the newer textbooks, try Donald J. Mastronarde's *Introduction to Attic Greek* or *Athenaze: An Introduction to Ancient Greek.*

This is also the time for the student to become familiar with alternative Greek pronunciation conventions. If the student has used the Erasmian pronunciation thus far, he should now familiarize himself with the reconstructed Attic pronunciation. Students who have used the ethnic pronunciation in their *koine* studies will want to learn Erasmian now. As a rule, the older textbooks use Erasmian, while more recent authors prefer reconstructed Attic.

Toward the end of tenth grade, the student can try her hand at translating simple texts from an anthology like Freeman and Lowe's **Greek Reader for Schools** (ISBN 0865162670), which includes selections from Aesop, Plato, and other authors.

Plan to spend at least two hours, twice a week on Greek at this level.

Eleventh Grade

The standard first "real" Greek text is Xenophon's **Anabasis** ("The Upland March"), the exciting chronicle of a Greek general trying to escape with his army of mercenaries from enemy territory after a failed coup. It is available in a popular student version, edited by Mather and Hewitt (ISBN 0806113472). Plan to complete at least Book I this year. If the student enjoys Xenophon, he may wish to read more in Greek, or follow up with a translation to find out how this action-packed story ends.

If you have chosen the *koine* option, you will be able to roll your Greek study together with Christian Studies this year by having your student read and translate the Gospel of John. Study notes are available at www.btinternet.com/~MisPar/GNotes/john.htm .

Twelfth Grade

If the student has persevered with Greek to this point, she now receives the great reward: the ability to read Homer in the original. Spend this year delighting in Benner's standard student edition, **Selections from Homer's Iliad** (ISBN 0806133635). *Homeric Greek: A Book for Beginners* by Pharr (ISBN 0806119373), *Homeric Vocabularies* (ISBN 0806108282) and *Lexicon of the Homeric Dialect* (ISBN 0806114304) are three standard resources to help your student master Homeric grammar and vocabulary.

Koine students can again roll Greek together with Christian Studies by reading and translating the Epistle to the Romans. Study notes are at: www.btinternet.com/~MisPar/GNotes/romans.htm .

VI. ARITHMETIC & MATHEMATICS

Let no one who is ignorant of geometry enter here.
—Inscription over the door of Plato's Academy

ℰℛ

Mathematics, along with the classical languages, forms the core of the classical curriculum; math represents the Quadrivium as Latin does the Trivium. Math is, therefore, your other daily discipline. Plan to spend 15-30 minutes on arithmetic in the primary-school years, working up to an hour by the end of grammar school. During this time, your goal is to have the student master arithmetic facts and processes (addition, subtraction, multiplication, division, fractions, decimals, etc.). In secondary school, the student's attention turns to two major mathematical disciplines: algebra and Euclidean geometry. Some students—especially those who expect to pursue advanced math or science studies in college—will want to continue through twelfth grade with pre-calculus and calculus. Expect to devote an hour or more a day to math; this may be arranged in several longer sessions two or three times a week.

Curriculum Overview

	Primary and Grammar School	Secondary School
Goals	Mastery of arithmetic facts and operations	Mastery of geometry and algebra; optional study of pre-calculus/calculus
Materials	Rod & Staff, Ray's, or curriculum of your choice; manipulatives; "living math" books	Euclid's *Elements*, Ray's *Plane and Solid Geometry, Elementary Algebra*, and *Higher Algebra*, or curriculum of your choice

Arithmetic in the Primary-School Years (K-2)

During these early years, focus on basic skills: counting, working with money, telling time, measuring, and learning simple addition and subtraction facts.

Kindergarten

Beginning in kindergarten—as early as age four—you can use preschool/K math programs like Singapore Early Bird Mathematics or Right Start. Singapore is a good choice for those who want to use a single curriculum through Secondary School. Alternatively, you can teach the basic skills with a 100-bead abacus or simple manipulatives (pennies, beans, candies) that you have at home. If you prefer not to use a formal math curriculum at this stage, you can invest in one wonderful book: Ruth Beechick's *An Easy Start in Arithmetic,* part of her Three R's collection (ISBN 0940319063), which includes a "100 chart." Games like pattern blocks, dominoes, cards, or dice can help reinforce mathematical concepts.

First and Second Grades

If you've chosen Singapore or Right Start, you can follow their sequence in these years. Otherwise, begin with **Rod & Staff's Mathematics for Christian Living Series, Ray's Primary Arithmetic,** or another program that emphasizes memorization and drill.

Ray's Primary Arithmetic can be used for both years. The entire Ray's series, which includes calculus and even astronomy and navigation, is available on CD-ROM from raysarithmetic.com at an attractive price. Rod & Staff's first grade book is called **Beginning Arithmetic**; the second-grade text is **Working Arithmetic.** Rod & Staff does not have a Web site but can be reached at (606) 522-4348 and will send free curriculum samples and scope-and-sequence charts to you upon request.

If you do choose Singapore, you may find that you need to supplement it with additional drills to assure that your student is mastering the necessary math facts. Use oral chants, drills from Ray's or Rod & Staff (the latter sells "black lines"—photocopy masters—of their drill sheets), flash cards, tabletop or computer math games, inexpensive workbooks like the McGraw-Hill Spectrum series, homemade worksheets, or some combination of these.

Arithmetic in the Grammar-School Years (3-8)

During these years it is crucial that the student master the basic skills begun in the primary-school years. Ignore grade levels and focus on skills, not moving forward until your student has mastered the material at each level.

Third-Eighth Grades

Follow the progression in your program of choice, adding extra drill, manipulatives, or math games as needed, until your student knows her facts cold. Generally each of the Ray's books—**Intellectual Arithmetic, Practical Arithmetic,** and **Higher Arithmetic** can be used for two years in these grades. Information about Ray's Arithmetic is available at raysarithmetic.com. Rod & Staff publishes one book per grade: **Exploring Arithmetic** (third), **Progressing in Arithmetic** (fourth), **Gaining Skill in Arithmetic** (fifth), **Understanding Numbers** (sixth), **Mastering Numbers** (seventh), and **Applying Numbers** (eighth). Teacher's manuals and black lines (photocopy masters for drill) are available. A complete scope-and-sequence for the Rod & Staff program can be had upon request by calling the company at (606) 522-4348.

Include a generous selection of math-related stories and biographies in your student's independent reading time, and enjoy games and puzzles as a family. Many resources for "living math" books can be found at livingmath.net .

Mathematics in the Secondary-School Years (9-12)

Here we begin the study of mathematics proper. All college-bound students will want to complete courses in algebra and geometry by the end of eleventh grade as these subjects figure prominently on the PSAT. Students who intend to pursue a major in a math- or science-related subject, or who hope to gain admission to a highly selective college, would do well to continue on to pre-calculus and calculus.

Ideally students would spend two years, ninth and tenth grade, studying Euclid, but unfortunately this would put college-bound students at a disadvantage on the PSAT, which assumes two years of algebra and one of geometry. Parents will have to weigh the advantages of longer geometry study. The course of study below assumes that standardized tests are a concern and allots study time accordingly.

If you have been using Singapore or Ray's, you can simply continue on with the sequence, taking time for a reading of the first book of Euclid's *Elements* when you reach the study of geometry. Rod & Staff's sequence ends in eighth grade.

Curriculum Overview

	Ninth Grade	Tenth Grade	Eleventh Grade	Twelfth Grade
Goals	Mastery of Plane Geometry	Mastery of Algebra I	Mastery of Algebra II (including Trigonometry)	Optional Study of Pre-Calculus
Materials	Euclid's *Elements*	Ray's *Elementary Algebra*, or curriculum of your choice	Ray's *Elementary Algebra* and/or *Higher Algebra*, or curriculum of your choice	Ray's *Differential and Integral Calculus* or community college class

Ninth Grade

The standard mathematics sequence in US schools dictates that students take Algebra I in ninth grade. If you are concerned about testing, you may wish to follow this sequence as well. If so, you can begin your ninth grader with **Ray's Elementary Algebra** this year and complete it (or continue on to *Higher Algebra*) in eleventh grade.

My preferred method, however, is to devote ninth grade to a careful reading of the first book of **Euclid's Elements,** working through each proof until the student can reproduce it independently. Some of the reading can be undertaken in Greek, even at this level. You may want to keep a geometry textbook (Ray's **Plane and Solid Geometry**, for example) or an SAT math prep book on hand so that your student is comfortable with the kinds of questions that appear on standardized tests. The student should also learn about some of the major figures in ancient geometry (Pythagoras and Euclid himself) and its role in philosophy (Plato).

For Parents:

For help with combining Greek and Geometry, visit the online "Greek for Euclid" course at www.du.edu/~etuttle/classics/nugreek/contents.htm .

Tenth and Eleventh Grades

If you are using the recommended sequence, your student will now begin two years' study of algebra using Ray's **Elementary Algebra** and **Higher Algebra,** or other texts of your choice. This will still put the student on track for standardized tests, but does not interrupt the logical flow of the subject as the conventional school sequence does. Again, make an effort to include some readings in the history of mathematics to show the student how the subject relates to the larger philosophical concerns of the curriculum: What is Man? What is the Good Life? How then shall we live?

Twelfth Grade

Students with an interest in math or science can continue on to pre-calculus and calculus using Ray's **Differential and Integral Calculus** or another book. Parents may wish to enroll the student in a community college class or find a tutor if their own math skills do not include these subjects and they are unable to study them in advance of their student. If your student is serious about applying to a highly selective college or university, you should be aware that these schools expect four years of the core subjects, including math. Selective liberal arts colleges are often satisfied with three years, particularly if the student is heading toward a degree in the humanities. Again, make time for the study of the history of calculus—a relatively new branch of mathematics—and for exploration of some of the contemporary concerns of the field.

For Parents:

Morris Kline, *Mathematics for the Nonmathematician* (ISBN 0486248232). This inexpensive Dover paperback is a college-level text that provides the cultural and historical context for math. It contains exercises (including essay questions), topics for further study, and suggestions for further reading—this last being rather out-of-date. It also discusses scientific applications of math, logic, and even art (e.g., a chapter on mathematics and painting in the Renaissance). An excellent resource for integrated math and the humanities.

VII. ENGLISH STUDIES

Distringit librorum multitudo. —**Seneca the Younger***

❧

English Studies corresponds to the sequence of grammar and rhetoric pursued in the ancient schools. It includes a number of distinct areas of study: reading and orthography; language mechanics and usage; English grammar—learned first through the medium of Latin; the *progymnasmata* (composition exercises); classical rhetoric and oratory; and the study of literature in English. Its aim is mastery of the mother tongue.

Areas of Study: An Overview

Before we look at specific curriculum suggestions for each grade, it may be helpful to get an overview of the English Studies curriculum as a whole. Although making Latin the core of your language arts program will eliminate the need for separate vocabulary and grammar curricula, English Studies still encompasses a wider range of areas than any other subject. Moreover, the skills you will focus on change dramatically as the student moves from the primary years into the Grammar School and on into Secondary School. These transitions are shown in the chart below. The following sections will take up each component of the subject individually, more or less in the order you will encounter them in the curriculum.

---

* "The availability of so many books is distracting."

Components of the English Studies Curriculum by Age

Primary School	Grammar School	Secondary School
* Phonics	* Literature Selections	* Literature Selections (plus
* Penmanship and	(read aloud by student	relevant critical sources)
Copywork	and parent)	* Discussion and Essays
* Recitation (Memory	* Discussion and Oral	* Independent Reading
Work)	Narration	* Family Reading
* Independent Reading	* Independent Reading	* Recitation/Oratory
* Literature Selections	* Family Reading	* Classical Rhetoric
(read aloud by parent)	* Copywork	
* Family Reading	* Recitation	
	* Progymnasmata	
	* English Grammar,	
	Usage, and Reading	
	Skills (8th Grade)	

Reading Instruction: Phonics

Reading instruction begins with one word: phonics. This is one thing all classical educators agree upon. Indeed, the ancients pioneered the incremental study of phonics in their schools:

> Instruction was based on a logical and orderly progression from letters to syllables, from syllables to words, and from words to sentences and short continuous passages.[93]

In an ancient Roman school, the alphabet might be learned by means of a poem, not unlike our ABC song, and students might be given a set of ivory or boxwood letters to help them recognize and form the shapes. Writing was practiced on wax tablets, following a light outline made by

93. Bonner, p. 165.

the teacher. Syllables were taught with equal care, with students reciting and writing each possible consonant and vowel combination: b, a, ba; b, e, be; and so on. From there, the students formed longer syllables (b, a, n, ban; b, e, n, ben), then single-syllable and finally multi-syllable words. The teacher would give exercises in some of the more difficult combinations, sometimes in the form of tongue-twisters, to help pupils pronounce words like *Thrax* (Thracian) or *lynx*. Vocabulary and spelling were taught by means of word lists, often containing historical or mythological names that the student would later encounter in his literary studies. Copywork was a mainstay of the curriculum, and teachers took pains to assure that the material written was both linguistically and morally sound, with proverbs and maxims figuring prominently.[94]

What can we glean from these methods? While we need not adopt ancient pedagogical practices uncritically, there is much to be said for the ancients' approach to reading and writing. That approach is incremental, systematic, and thorough. This much we can surely imitate.

Modern students will also benefit from some of the ancient methods, including the use of letter blocks (perhaps borrowed from your family's Scrabble set) or cards (from the game Quiddler), songs, and tongue-twisters. More will be said about specific curricula and copywork shortly.

Independent Reading and Family Reading

As soon as possible, students should begin to read on their own. This doesn't mean that you stop reading to them, only that they should undertake periods of sustained silent reading daily. New readers may reach their frustration threshold in a few minutes, but you can expect early-grammar students to read for a minimum of 30 minutes a day. That time should increase to an hour by sixth grade. I suggest that stu-

---

94. Bonner, pp. 166-176.

dents be allowed to choose their own independent reading from a list of parent-approved books. (Parents will need to determine their own policies regarding other reading material.)

In addition to this independent reading, I strongly urge you to make a habit of family reading, either in the evenings, during a quiet hour in the afternoon, or even over breakfast—whenever you can assemble your family in one place. This is the time to establish a lifelong love of literature and to enjoy all those beloved English-language classics together.

When choosing reading material, it is vital to avoid what British classical educator Charlotte Mason called "twaddle." At its most obvious, twaddle is characterized by inane plots, insipid characters, poor vocabulary, and simplistic syntax; and by cartoonish, ugly, or grotesque pictures. Unfortunately, many children's books and virtually all contemporary young adult fiction titles are twaddle. Please do preview the books your children read and do not assume that books your children's friends enjoy or the local librarian considers appropriate will be acceptable to you on aesthetic, intellectual, or moral grounds.

When selecting books, look for three things: literary language; worthy stories and characters; and quality illustrations. Ask yourself, "Does this story ennoble the child's mind? Does it speak to his heart? What aesthetic, intellectual, and moral models does it place before her? Will he be a better person for having read it?"

Feel free to explore the many wonderful picture books and children's classics available at your local library. Extensive lists of outstanding fiction and nonfiction titles can be found in *Honey for a Child's Heart, The Well-Trained Mind, Books to Build On,* the Veritas Press catalog, the Highlands Latin School's summer reading lists, and Web sites too numerous to list. Don't be afraid to let young children listen in on family read-alouds chosen with older children in mind. Children are able to enjoy literature far beyond their own reading level, and their education is enriched by getting to know the classics early. It is helpful to remember that the early American colonists learned to read with little more than a hornbook and a Bible—and not an illustrated children's story Bible either!

Appendix A provides some suggestions for independent and family reading that correspond to the main literature selections and assigned reading in other subjects.

Penmanship and Copywork

Copywork—writing a "fair copy" after a literary model—is decidedly out of fashion in most schools, but classical educators still champion the method. Students learn by imitation, particularly in these early years, so it stands to reason that we should place the best models before them. Copywork provides training in penmanship and its handmaiden skills—small motor control, neatness, patience, and precision. It is also the student's first hands-on experience with correct spelling, punctuation, and usage. If the model sentences are well chosen, copywork will also begin to stock the child's mind with edifying and uplifting thoughts and useful facts.

Recitation

Closely related to copywork is recitation, or memory work, as it is sometimes called. It was not for nothing that the ancient Greeks called Memory the mother of the Muses! Children's capacity for memorization is nothing short of astonishing to us adults, but we should not underestimate it or let the opportunity it presents slip by. From the earliest years we can provide our children with intellectual and spiritual nourishment in the form of poems, prayers, Scripture, or catechism. In the grammar-school years we expand the range of poetic choices, and still later, add oratory in the form of speeches and dramatic selections. As

Quintilian observed, we must be aware that:

> ...these tender minds, which will be deeply affected by whatever is impressed upon them in their untrained ignorance, should learn not only eloquent passages but, even more, passages which are morally improving.

Literature

The study of great works of literature is one of the key components of English Studies. By applying the *multum non multa* principle to the English curriculum, we focus on a small number of recognized masterpieces—works that have shaped our culture in fundamental ways.

Literature in the Primary Years

In the primary years, the goal is to familiarize children with some of the foundational stories of our culture: Biblical narratives, fairy tales, folk tales, nursery rhymes, tall tales, fables, legends, and myths. These simple stories, through sheer repetition, sink into the children's minds, nourishing them intellectually and spiritually.

Teaching Literature in the Grammar Years

As students grow, our teaching method must grow with them. The ancients developed a standard approach to teaching their culture's masterworks to the young. Quintilian, for example, tells us that teachers should instruct their students about meter, the parts of speech, unusual words (barbarisms), poetic and rhetorical devices, and the organization and propriety of the subject matter, as well as explaining historical and mythological allusions. This all seems a bit stiff for the third grade! But again, we can take from these methods some cues for our own teaching, particularly in the late-grammar and secondary years.

Plan to read the literature selections aloud, taking turns with your student. Why undertake this time-consuming task, when the student is capable of reading the books to himself? There are several reasons. Some of the literature selections—especially the plays and poetry—were meant to be performed orally, and doing so allows for greater appreciation of the work's original context and artistry. In addition, it is often easier for students to parse complex syntax and vocabulary when they hear a passage read aloud, with proper inflection. They can also stop and inquire right away about the meaning of unfamiliar words, constructions, or references—"Wait, who is he talking about there?"—and parents can check instantly for comprehension.

But there is another reason for preferring oral performance to silent reading. We have already seen that the ancient schools required copious oral reading as a preparation for rhetoric. More recent research has confirmed what they knew: Students who consistently hear correct and elegant language are better able to produce it on their own. Andrew Pudewa addresses this issue in his article "One Myth, Two Truths."[95] He notes that good writers are those who are able "to communicate ideas in understandable, reliably correct, appropriately sophisticated language patterns." Contrary to popular opinion, it is not always the avid early readers who are best able to do this:

> Good readers read quickly, silently and aggressively. They don't audiate (hear internally) each word or even complete sentences. Generally, comprehension increases with speed, but speed decreases language pattern audiation because good readers will skip words, phrases and even complete sections of books that might

95. http://www.memoriapress.com/articles/One-Myth.html

hold them back. And to the extent that children don't hear—frequently—a multitude of complete reliably correct and sophisticated language patterns, such patterns are not going to be effectively stored in their brains.[96]

Pudewa suggests two practical solutions to this problem: recitation and listening—being read to aloud.

In addition to understanding the meaning and syntax of their reading, students need context to make sense of literature. We have seen that ancient grammar teachers lectured on the literature they taught, explaining references and context. Who is the author? When did he or she live, and where? What do we know about the author's life? Today, we can provide the same for our students. Placing the author on a timeline and reading a short biographical sketch make a good start. Next, the student needs an entrée into the story itself: Where and when is it set? Who are the main characters? What is the main thrust of the narrative? It may be helpful to read (and to have your student read) a plot summary or list of characters before plunging into the work itself. Far from ruining the experience of reading, this background knowledge saves students from the frustration that so many encounter when they first approach authors like Homer or Shakespeare. Do not be afraid to turn to Cliff Notes or classicnotes.com for this sort of information. You might also consider watching documentaries or dramatizations to enrich your child's understanding of the author, period, or plot.

For works with many characters, like the *Iliad*, it will be helpful to make a list with the student of the characters and the various ways they are referred to. Who is "the son of Peleus"? Where do the Achaians come from? What is the relationship between Achilles and Patroclus? Related to these questions are the poetic conventions of a particular author or genre. Why do we encounter repeated phrases like "rosy-fingered Dawn" and "wine-dark sea" in Homer? Mythological and historical references

---

96. In: *The Classical Teacher*, Winter 2005, pp. 22-23.

also need to be explained: Why do the Greeks speak of Dawn as a person? Which side do the various Olympians take in the Trojan war, and why? Where was Mycenae? Troy?

Clearly, as teachers, parents will need to be prepared to teach this material actively, not just hand it to their students to read. This is another great advantage of the *multum non multa* principle: If your student is only reading a few books a year, you have more time to prepare to teach them in depth. Do read ahead, scour your library for secondary sources on the literature selections, make friends with the reference librarians and interlibrary loan people, and be willing to do the legwork to make your child's experience of these literary masterpieces as rich as possible. I have listed a few key resources after the literature selections for each year to get you started.

Discussion and Narration in the Grammar Years

How do you know if your students are understanding Homer or Shakespeare? Ask them! Talk with them about the plot, and ask them to narrate, in their own words, what has happened in the story so far. If they mention a character's name, you can say, "Which one was she again?" If they don't know the answer, look it up together. In the early grammar years, you are looking for simple comprehension of the narrative: What? Who? When? Where? Late-grammar students can begin to discuss poetic conventions and character motivation (*"How* do you think Achilles felt about the way Menelaus spoke to him? *Why* do you think he responded the way he did?"). In seventh or eighth grade, students can begin reading critical essays on the literature selections.

Although your student will be getting plenty of practice with writing in their composition curriculum, you may want to ask them to demonstrate the techniques learned in the *progymnasmata* by writing plot summaries, mock speeches, or maxims derived from their literature readings. ("If you could give Achilles a piece of advice right before he goes off to slay Paris, what would it be?"; "What is the moral of the *Odyssey*?")

Teaching Literature in the Secondary Years

By the time students have reached ninth grade, they will be well prepared to tackle the secondary-school literature curriculum. They will already have studied several substantial works of literature; they will have completed the *progymnasmata;* they will be starting the study of formal rhetoric. The goal in these years is to read slowly, to dig deep into the works, and to write clearly about what one discovers there.

To that end, we add two components to literature studies at this stage. First, students should begin writing essays regularly. (More on that in a moment.) Second, they should be reading some literary criticism alongside their literature selections and responding to the ideas they find there in their essays. This is the essence of college-level literature studies, and any student who becomes comfortable with the process in secondary school will derive more benefit from college instruction than those who come less prepared.

I again suggest that the students read the literature selections aloud whenever possible. This is particularly important for the plays (Shakespeare and also the Greek tragedies read in Classical Studies), for epic (*Beowulf*), and for lyric poetry. You may also want to seek out audio books or video productions to supplement the student's reading.

Composition: The Progymnasmata

This brings us to the discussion of composition as a component of the English Studies curriculum. The ancient schools were not limited to the study of literature for its own sake. The goal of rhetorical education was practical: to enable young men to take their places in public life, in the government and the law courts. A command of the written and spoken languages was therefore vital to the success of the rhetorical program—and the lives of the students.

Consequently, the ancient Greeks developed a carefully graded set of composition exercises to prepare students for the study of formal rhetoric. Known as the *progymnasmata,* these preliminary exercises formed the basis of writing instruction for both the Greek and the Romans. Like phonics instruction, they moved from the simple to the more complex. Like literary study, they relied on models of moral and aesthetic excellence to train students' minds and spirits.

Although the exact order of the exercises varied from author to author, they generally included the following:

1. Fable
2. Narrative
3. Chreia (moral anecdote)
4. Maxim
5. Refutation
6. Confirmation
7. Commonplace
8. Encomium and Invective (praise and blame)
9. Comparison
10. Speech-in-Character
11. Description
12. Thesis
13. Laws

Within each exercise the student learned techniques such as the ordering of information and the use of figures of speech. They also analyzed examples of each form before imitating it themselves.

Happily for us home schoolers, the *progymnasmata* form the basis of several excellent composition curricula, discussed below.

Rhetoric and Essays

Having completed the *progymnasmata* in the grammar-school years, the student is now prepared to study formal rhetoric. Ninth grade is devoted to a program designed to take the student through Aristotle's *Rhetoric*, which will solidify and refine his writing skills.

Mastering those skills requires diligence and much practice. I recommend that secondary-school students write essays on a set schedule. In ninth grade, *Classical Rhetoric with Aristotle* will provide abundant material for essay writing. Beginning in tenth grade, students should be writing at least two short essays a month, on topics of the teacher's choosing, related to their reading in English Studies, Modern Studies, and Classical and Christian Studies. By eleventh grade, the student should be completing one five-paragraph essay a week, and in twelfth grade, these essays should be timed. (Allow 45 minutes per essay.) Finally, I encourage you to assign at least two major research papers on literary or historical topics of interest to the student, perhaps one each in eleventh and twelfth grades. This work is particularly important for college-bound students who will find that the bulk of their work in the humanities consists of research and writing about what they have read for class.

Now that we've surveyed the English Studies terrain, let's look at curriculum suggestions for each year.

English Studies in the Primary-School Years (K-2)

For the primary-age student, the goal is fluency in reading. This is achieved through a thorough, incremental study of phonics. Orthography—which includes penmanship, writing conventions, and spelling—is approached through copywork. Students are introduced to literature by listening to books written at an elevated level of vocabulary and sentence structure, and through increasing amounts of independent reading of high-quality children's books. Finally, regular recitation exercises the students' memories and stocks their minds with beautiful language and ennobling thoughts.

The components of the primary-school English Studies curriculum are (1) Phonics; (2) Penmanship and Copywork; (3) Recitation (Memory Work); (4) Literature Selections (read aloud by parent); (5) Independent Reading; and (6) Family Reading.

Phonics in the Primary-School Years

As we have seen, the ancients were highly systematic in the teaching of reading. They worked deliberately from parts to whole, first introducing letters, then syllables, and finally words. In other words, they used what we call "phonics" today.

Simple programs like **Phonics Pathways** (ISBN 0962096733) move the student systematically from letters to syllables to three-letter (consonant-vowel-consonant) words to blends to polysyllabic words. If you prefer a scripted method, **The Ordinary Parent's Guide to Teaching Reading** (ISBN 0972860312) will appeal. Since English phonetics are rather more complicated that those of Latin or Greek, the practice of learning phonemes also has much to recommend it, particularly as an aid to spelling. **The Writing Road to Reading** (ISBN 0060520108), also known as the Spalding method, takes this approach. Finally, Ruth Beechick's affordable **A Home Start in Reading** (part of her Three R's package, ISBN 0940319063) gives parents the tools to create their own phonics program.

Plan to spend 15-30 minutes a day on phonics. Slow and steady is the rule.

Penmanship and Copywork for the Primary-School Years

In kindergarten, we begin writing as we did reading: with letters, then syllables, then words, and finally sentences. I recommend that students learn Italic handwriting from the start. Not only does Italic encourage tidy, legible, beautiful writing, but it also eliminates the need to learn a whole new cursive alphabet at a later stage.

The most straightforward handwriting curriculum I have found is **Italics: Beautiful Handwriting for Children** by Penny Gardner (available from pennygardner.com). This affordable student worktext may be used throughout the primary-school years. An alternative is the Getty-Dubay Italic series. Graded workbooks are available for kindergarten through sixth grade, and parents who want a reference guide can turn to the authors' adult program, **Write Now.** For additional practice, you can purchase a font based on Getty-Dubay Italic as part of the home schoolers' package from Educational Fontware (www.educationalfontware.com).

Memoria Press has recently satisfied the need for copywork materials with the publication of Leigh Lowe's K-2 **Copybooks.** These include selections of Scripture and poetry; the handwriting style used is similar to D'Nealian. Other sources for copywork texts include scripture, proverbs, prayers, and poetry. One convenient collection of KJV Bible quotations for copywork is **Bible Quotes for Phonics, Copywork, and Spelling** (JoyceHerzog.com), but any list of well-known verses will serve. Look for poetry selections in the indispensable **Harp and Laurel Wreath** by Laura Berquist (ISBN 0898707161) or in your favorite anthology. As students progress in their studies, copywork should include material in Latin and Greek. A large selection of Latin sayings with English translations can be found in **Latin Proverbs: Wisdom from Ancient to Modern Times** (bolchazy.com) and online at www.mythfolklore.net/calendars/latin/latinprovs.htm (no translations are provided). The prayers and Latin phrases in *Prima Latina* and *Latina Christiana* may also be used. **Greek Proverbs** (ISBN 0862815568) contains a nice selection of maxims in ancient Greek, modern Greek, and English, and a selection (without translations) is also available online at www.mythfolklore.net/calendars/greek/greekprovs.htm .

Copywork should be practiced every school day, but it is not necessary to spend more than five or ten minutes on it, particularly for the youngest children.

Recitation in the Primary-School Years

Any text that you use for copywork will also serve for recitation. Begin with simple rhymes, perhaps from Mother Goose or folk songs. Traditional children's prayers ("Now I lay me down to sleep"), basic religious affirmations (the Gloria Patri, the Shema, etc.), and short passages of Scripture also make good subjects for recitation. **The Harp and Laurel Wreath** contains a generous selection of materials for recitation, arranged by age.

Literature in the Primary-School Years

During these years, the goal is to immerse children in the foundational stories of our culture, including familiar Bible stories, fairy tales, legends, myths, and poems. The literature selections nurture the child's imagination and spirit, as well as introducing simple literary forms, such as the fable and the tall tale.

Literature Selections for Kindergarten

Nursery Rhymes. Look for a generous, well-illustrated collection with fairly large type like *Mother Goose: The Original Volland Edition* (ISBN 0517436191), *The Real Mother Goose* (ISBN 0590225170), or *The Original Mother Goose* (ISBN 1561381136).

Nursery Tales. Simple, humorous tales like "The Gingerbread Man," "The Three Little Pigs," and "Goldilocks and the Three Bears" are well suited to this age. Choose a collection like *The Random House Book of Nursery Stories* (ISBN 0375805869) or *Great Children's Stories: The Classic Volland Edition* (ISBN 0516098837), or check your library for individual picture books.

Read these tales frequently, and ask your child to tell them back to you. Try different picture-book versions from the public library. Tell the stories in your own words, putting your child into the story. Sing nursery rhymes as you go about your household tasks, or invest in a tape of nursery songs. Not only are these stories and rhymes a precious part of childhood, but they encourage play with language—the very sort of play that we find in our great poets. Even they once sang "Hickory, Dickory, Dock."

The following tales should form the core of your reading, but feel free to read whatever strikes your fancy, or your child's.

The Gingerbread Man
The Three Little Pigs
The Magic Cooking Pot (called "Sweet Porridge" by the Grimms; Tomie dePaola's *Strega Nona* is a modern retelling of this story)
The Little Red Hen
Goldilocks and the Three Bears

The Turnip

The Three Billy Goats Gruff

Chicken Little (also known as Henny Penny)

The Bremen Town-Musicians

Literature Selections for First Grade

Fifty Famous Stories Retold. This wonderful collection of histories and legends by James Baldwin is back in print from Yesterday's Classics (lulu.com) and is also available online at mainlesson.com. This book is also used in the second grade; you need only read the first half of the book this year.

Fairy Tales. Invest in well-illustrated editions of Grimms' and Hans Christian Andersen's tales. Dover Publications offers an inexpensive edition of the Grimms' tales under the title *Household Stories by the Brothers Grimm* (ISBN 0486210804), nicely illustrated by Walter Crane. Arthur Rackham's illustrations of the Grimms' fairy tales are justifiably famous, but not always easy to find in print. Explore the beautiful picture book editions by illustrators like K. Y. Craft (*Sleeping Beauty, The Twelve Dancing Princesses, Cinderella*) and Paul O. Zelinsky (*Rapunzel, Rumpelstiltskin, Hansel and Gretel*). *Fairy Tales from Hans Christian Andersen* (ISBN 0811802302) contains the major tales and beautiful illustrations. The collections by Andrew Lang (*The Red Fairy Book, The Blue Fairy Book,* etc.) are also delightful sources of tales, both well known and rare. All twelve of Lang's fairy books can also be found online at www.mythfolklore.net/andrewlang/ .

The following familiar tales should form the core of your reading, but don't miss some of the less familiar stories:

Snow White

Cinderella

Rapunzel

Hansel and Gretel

The Frog Prince

The Fisherman and His Wife

The Valiant Little Tailor

Mother Holle

Little Red Riding Hood

Briar Rose (Sleeping Beauty)

Rumpelstiltskin

The Golden Goose

Snow White and Rose Red

Hans the Hedgehog

Iron Hans (Iron John)

The Star Money

Puss in Boots (by Perrault)

Beauty and the Beast

The Pied Piper of Hamelin

Tom Thumb (Thumbling)

The Little Mermaid

Thumbelina

The Ugly Duckling

The Little Match Girl

The Tinder Box

The Fir-Tree

The Steadfast Tin Soldier

The Real Princess (The Princess and the Pea)

The Emperor's New Clothes

Literature Selections for Second Grade

Fifty Famous Stories Retold. Available from Yesterday's Classics (lulu.com) and free online at mainlesson.com. Read the second half of the book this year.

Folk Tales. Folk tales and legends—often with a humorous touch—have a great appeal to children of this age and can also teach important lessons. I recommend two collections: *American Tall Tales* by Mary Pope Osborne (ISBN 0679800891) and *The Tales of Uncle Remus: The Adventures of Brer Rabbit,* retold by Julius Lester and illustrated by Jerry Pinkney (ISBN 0141303476). The unabridged cassette version of the latter (ISBN 0788753622), read by Professor Lester, is outstanding. This talented team has also brought out a moving picture book version of the John Henry story (ISBN 0140566228). If you prefer individual picture books on characters like Davy Crockett, Johnny Appleseed, and Paul Bunyan, look for titles by Steven Kellogg. Finally, Amy L. Cohn's *From Sea to Shining Sea: A Treasury of American Folklore and Folk Songs* (ISBN 0590428683) makes a useful addition to help you integrate music into your English studies. It also contains many stories and can serve as an alternative to Osborne.

Independent Reading in the Primary-School Years

Once students have mastered three-letter words with short vowels, they can begin to read the ubiquitous **Bob Books** (bobbooks.com). While these little books can be maddening to parents in their repetitive simplicity, they provide wonderful practice for beginning readers and build confidence as well as skills. Unless you have many children, it is not worth buying these, as your beginning reader will not stay with them long. Instead, borrow them from the library or a friend.

From there, the student can progress to graded early readers and classic picture books. These need not be the monotonous, canned prose of Dick and Jane. Perennial favorites such as Dr. Seuss, Frog and Toad, or Little Bear make great stepping-stones. You may also want to look at the book lists for programs like Five in a Row (fiveinarow.com), Sonlight (sonlight.com), Veritas Press's Kindergarten and First Grade selections (veritaspress.com), or the Year 0 list from Ambleside Online (ambleside-online.org). In addition, many lists of excellent picture books can be found online, such as the "1000 Good Books" list from the Classical Christian Education Support Loop (www.classical-homeschooling.org/celoop/1000.html).

Family Reading in the Primary-School Years

This is the time to enjoy all the classics you remember from your own childhood—or the ones you wish you'd read! Beatrix Potter's stories, the Pooh books, *The Wind in the Willows, Mary Poppins, Little House in the Big Woods, Farmer Boy, Just So Stories, The Jungle Book, Pinocchio*…So many books, so little time! Make that time. Your children will thank you. For a wonderful list of children's classics, visit www.schoolofabraham.com/goodbooks.htm .

English Studies in the Grammar School Years (3-8)

The twin pursuits for the grammar-school years are (1) the slow, in-depth reading of a thoughtful selection of classic stories and poems in English, and (2) preparation for formal rhetoric by means of the carefully graded ancient composition exercises known as the *progymnasmata*. The material read corresponds to studies in other subject areas, such as Modern Studies, Christian Studies, and Classical Studies.

Students demonstrate their comprehension of the literature selections through guided discussions with the parent-teacher and oral narration. In the late-grammar years, you may also want to integrate literature studies and composition by asking for an occasional short written narration (précis) or simple essay.

In addition to the time spent studying the literature selections, the student should be reading independently, choosing from a list drawn up by the parents, for at least 30 minutes a day in third grade, working up to an hour in the sixth grade and beyond. Family read-alouds of an hour a day are desirable. Copywork and recitation continue, with the student memorizing at least three or four poems a year.

Literature in the Grammar-School Years

Rather than spending these years studying contemporary children's fiction or even fine classics like *Little Women* or *Treasure Island,* students read a small selection of challenging but age-appropriate literary masterpieces. At this stage most students will be able to read the books on their own, but I urge you to consider reading them aloud, in tandem—you read a few pages, then your student reads a few. These are books to be savored, and you will also find that complex syntax and unfamiliar vocabulary prove more accessible when read aloud.

For more information on how to use narration and discussion with grammar-age students, see page 95.

For Parents:

Louise Cowan and Os Guinness, eds., *Invitation to the Classics* (ISBN 0801011566). Short overviews of many Great Books, with author bios, plot summaries, bibliographies, and useful study questions and essay topics. Written from a Christian perspective, but mostly usable by non-Christians as well.

The Intercollegiate Studies Institute has published a series of guides to the core curriculum that give tips and secondary sources for studying many of the English Studies selections mentioned here. The books are available for purchase or for free download at www.isi.org/college_guide/home_schooling_resources.html .

Literature Selections for Third Grade

Nathaniel Hawthorne's *Wonder Book* and *Tanglewood Tales.* These two collections, by an American master, retell the Greek myths in a fresh and age-appropriate way, using Hawthorne's characteristically rich language.

Literature Selections for Fourth Grade

Lambs' *Tales from Shakespeare.* These faithful retellings of Shakespeare's finest plays are masterpieces in their own right. You may want to watch a few videos of the plays or listen to *Shakespeare's Greatest Hits,* from Full Cast Audio (www.fullcastaudio.com) to help your students appreciate the flavor of Elizabethan drama.

Literature Selections for Fifth Grade

William Shakespeare: *A Midsummer Night's Dream;* **Roger Lancelyn Green:** *King Arthur and His Knights of the Round Table;* **J. R. R. Tolkien:** *The Hobbit.* This year your student will explore fantasy and legend with three great storytellers. After the previous year's exposure to *Tales from Shakespeare,* your student is ready for her first full-fledged play, the charming and whimsical *Midsummer Night's Dream.* Green's retellings of the Arthurian legends are masterful, and no child should miss Bilbo's escapades. Don't forget your pocket handkerchief and remember: "Carefully, carefully with the plates!"

Literature Selections for Sixth Grade

The English and Classical Studies curricula are rolled together for sixth grade. See page 121 for details.

Literature Selections for Seventh Grade

The English and Classical Studies curricula are rolled together for seventh grade. See page 122 for details.

Literature Selections for Eighth Grade

J.R.R. Tolkien: *Lord of the Rings.* Widely regarded as the most enduring novel of the twentieth century, Tolkien's masterpiece brings together universal themes of heroism and redemption. *Literary Lessons from Lord of the Rings,* available from homescholar.org, is a complete literature curriculum based on the book and may prove helpful in studying this complex story. You may also want to have your student read a biography of Tolkien—Humphrey Carpenter's *J.R.R. Tolkien: A Biogra-*

phy (ISBN 0618057021) is the authorized one—and a selection of critical essays. The success of Peter Jackson's film versions has precipitated a veritable avalanche of Tolkien criticism. *Understanding the Lord of the Rings* (ISBN 061842251X), a collection of essays from a wide range of critical perspectives, and *Celebrating Middle-Earth* (ISBN 1587420139) are helpful guides to Tolkien's masterpiece and enlightening first introductions to literary criticism.

Additional Readings in Grammar and Literary Studies for Eighth Grade

Mortimer Adler and Charles Van Doren: *How to Read a Book.* This important guide will prepare the student for the intensive reading required in the secondary-school years. Although the book is fairly straightforward in its presentation, there is a study guide available that may prove helpful: *How to Read: How to Read a Book* by Maryalice B. Newborn (www.classicalhomeeducation.com).

Nancy Wilson: *Our Mother Tongue* and Strunk & White: *The Elements of Style*. Now that the student is completing the Latin grammar, it is time for a survey of English grammar and usage. Work through Wilson's exercises (the books and a key are available from canonpress.org) and commit as many of Strunk & White's rules to memory as possible.

Composition in the Grammar Years

Beginning in third grade, students take part in a real classical tradition: the carefully graded series of composition exercises known as the *progymnasmata*. As you will remember, these teach writing through the imitation of classical literary models such as fable, narrative, and maxim as they prepare the student for the study of formal rhetoric in secondary school.

For grammar-school students, there are currently two curriculum options: *Classical Writing* by Tracy Davis Gustilo and Lene Mahler Jaqua, and *Classical Composition* by Jim Selby. They take somewhat different approaches to the teaching of writing, and which you choose will depend largely on your own strengths and interests as a teacher. The cost of the two programs is comparable.

Classical Writing (www.classicalwriting.com) is a full language arts curriculum incorporating reading, word studies, copywork, dictation, and beginning with the second volume, formal English grammar. The authors recommend a total of one hour a day, four days a week to use the program. Currently there are three volumes available: *Classical Writing—Aesop*, which covers the fable portion of the *progymnasmata*, *Classical Writing—Homer* for narrative, and *Classical Writing—Poetry for Beginners*. Others are due out shortly. The authors maintain a Web site, a mailing list, and an online forum to support users of their program.

Classical Composition (www.classicalcomposition.com) focuses on writing only and does not incorporate formal English grammar instruction. The teacher's materials provide straightforward, detailed instruction for how to use the program. Each lesson is designed to be used over eight days, but these need not be consecutive, and students can easily move at their own pace. If used as described, the program might occupy 30 to 45 minutes each day of study. At this writing, Mr. Selby has published volumes on fable, narrative, chreia/maxim, refutation and confirmation, common topic, encomium, invective, and comparison. The remaining volumes are due out presently, and home school support services are also in the works. The materials come in loose-leaf binders; student workbooks are also available, although these are not necessary to teach the program.

If you have the time and confidence to design your own lesson plans and want a fully integrated language arts curriculum, you may prefer *Classical Writing*. If you are looking for a program that is straightforward and simple to implement and are not concerned about incorporating formal English grammar at this stage, then *Classical Composition* would be an excellent choice. The publishing schedule of the two programs will also be a consideration; as *Classical Writing* has only a few volumes available, parents with older students may opt for *Classical Composition*'s fuller program to assure that the material is available as their students need it. Both programs will give your child a strong foundation in writing and good preparation for the formal study of rhetoric at the secondary-school level.

For Parents:

Composition in the Classical Tradition by Frank J. D'Angelo (ISBN 0023271418). This detailed discussion of the *progymnasmata* is a helpful reference for parents. It can also be used as a textbook in the secondary-school years for students who have not studied the *progymnasmata* in grammar school.

Copywork in the Grammar-School Years

Copywork selections can be taken from the literature readings, from the *Harp & Laurel Wreath,* from Scripture, or from any poems selected for recitation. Aim for 10 minutes of copywork per day, in the student's best hand.

Recitation in the Grammar-School Years

Poems for recitation can be selected from the appropriate section of the *Harp & Laurel Wreath* or from one of the following poetry anthologies:

Philip Smith, ed., *100 Best-Loved Poems* (ISBN 0486285537)
William Harmon, ed., *The Classic Hundred Poems*, 2nd ed. (ISBN 0231112599)

There is a great deal of overlap between these two books, so it is not necessary to buy both. Suitable poems can also be found in standard anthologies like the *Norton Anthology of Poetry* or the *Oxford Book of English Verse*.

Note also that the recommended Modern Studies curriculum for these years, the *Artner Reader's Guide to American History*, suggests poems and other material for recitation, keyed to the historical period being studied. You may wish to incorporate this material into your English Studies recitations.

English Studies in the Secondary-School Years (9-12)

The program outlined below is designed to correspond to the Roman rhetoric school with its focus on formal rhetorical studies and intensive reading of a few representative literary masterpieces. In addition to his literature readings, the student studies classical rhetoric (Aristotle) as well as examples of outstanding speeches in Latin and English. The student continues to memorize and recite poems, and now adds speeches and dramatic selections to her repertoire.

Literature in the Secondary-School Years

In addition to several hours of independent and family reading a day, the student will continue to study, in depth, a small body of masterful literary works—novels, plays, and poetry—including works of world literature in translation.

Literature Selections for Ninth Grade

***Beowulf* (trans. Heaney), *Sir Gawain and the Green Knight* (trans. Tolkien), Chaucer's *Canterbury Tales* (selections from the *Norton Critical Edition*).** These three great classics will give your student a sense of the range of medieval literature in English. Do read Tolkien's introduction to his translation of *Sir Gawain* for the background and importance of the poem. You may also want to have your student read C. S. Lewis's introduction to medieval literature, *The Discarded Image* (ISBN 0521477352). Helen Cooper's *The Canterbury Tales* (ISBN 0198711557) will help you and your student with Chaucer. Be aware that some portions of Chaucer's text are earthy, to say the least. Do pre-read to determine which selections will best suit your family's needs.

Literature Selection for Tenth Grade

Dante: *The Divine Comedy* (Sayers translation preferred). Having delved into medieval English, the student now approaches what is arguably the greatest literary monument of medieval vernacular literature: *The Divine Comedy.* Let Joseph Gallagher be your Virgil as he guides you through Dante's creation with his *Modern Reader's Guide to Dante's the Divine Comedy* (ISBN 0764804944).

Literature Selections for Eleventh Grade

Shakespeare's plays. Students read a generous selection of the plays including comedies, tragedies, and histories. If you are unsure of which to choose, try revisiting the stories your student read back in fourth grade. Watch some of the many excellent video productions, patronize your local Shakespeare troupe—even small towns have them—and if at all possible, have your student take part in a production. At very least, find a group of like-minded home schoolers to perform the plays as readers' theater. The following books will help you and your student learn about the man, the stage, and the world of Elizabethan England: Dennis Kay, *William Shakespeare: His Life and Times* (ISBN 0805770631) and Andrew Gurr, *The Shakespearean Stage* (ISBN 052142240X). (Look for other titles by Gurr as well.)

Literature Selections for Twelfth Grade

English poetry. The student undertakes a survey of major English-language poets with special focus on poetic culture of 19th-century England (Coleridge, Blake, Byron, Shelley, Keats, Tennyson, Wordsworth). Choose either the *New Oxford Book of English Verse,* ed. Gardner (ISBN 0198121369) or *The Portable Romantic Poets,* ed. Auden & Pearson (ISBN 0140150528) as a starting point, and include at least one epic—perhaps Tennyson's *Idylls of the King.*

Rhetoric in the Secondary-School Years

In ninth grade, use Martin Cothran's **Classical Rhetoric with Aristotle** (www.memoriapress.com). This course guides the student through a close reading of Aristotle's *Rhetoric* and includes comprehension questions; weekly research and writing assignments; instruction on figures of speech with examples from a wide range of literary sources; a review of logic material from Mr. Cothran's Traditional Logic course (which students will have completed in the late grammar-school years); and case studies in rhetoric, including Shakespeare. In addition, Cothran integrates material from *How to Read a Book,* which I suggest students read in eighth grade. This is, then, an excellent course that synthesizes a great deal of material from previous years and also prepares the student for the research and essay-writing that will occupy them in the secondary-school years.

For Parents:

Classical Rhetoric for the Modern Student by Edward P. J. Corbett (ISBN 0195115422). Standard college-level rhetoric textbook. Useful as a reference for parents and may also be used as an advanced course in rhetoric for 11th or 12th graders.

Recitation and Oratory in the Secondary-School Years

Students continue to memorize poetry—particularly in twelfth grade when they are studying the English poets—but now add speeches from plays and history. Shakespeare is the obvious choice for the former; material from Modern Studies may supply the latter. *The Harp and Laurel Wreath* will again prove worth its weight in gold. During the eleventh grade, focus on the material in *Poetry for Young People: William Shakespeare* ed. David Scott Kastan & Marina Kastan (ISBN 0806943440).

If possible, arrange for your student to recite in public, perhaps by acting in a play or in a contest. Effective public speaking was, after all, one of the primary goals of ancient rhetorical education, and the lack of fine speakers among the current generation of world leaders shows the results of abandoning that educational tradition. Let your student be among those to redeem the time.

VIII. CLASSICAL STUDIES

A man who has not read Homer is like a man who has not seen the Ocean.

—Walter Bagehot

ഐ

If you turn back to the definition of "classical education" that I presented in the first chapter of this book, you'll see that it mentions classical languages and classical cultures. We've already looked in detail at the Latin and Greek languages. With Classical Studies, we turn to the cultures.*

Why devote so much attention these civilizations, so distant in time and place? Would it not be more sensible for our students' effort to be spent on studying our own culture?

While we certainly do need to learn about our own forms of government and more recent events, the history of education in the West has shown again and again the value of the ancients. Our own history is too close to us to allow for objectivity; we immediately become caught up in emotional response. Is a writer liberal or conservative? Were the Founders deeply Christian, or were they more swayed by Enlightenment thinking than by revelation? Is this piece of contemporary art worthy of our attention, let alone public funding? Is this textbook politically correct—and is that a good thing or a bad thing?

Although it is certainly possible to bring such topical concerns to our study of the ancients—as even a brief look at the sorts of books published by professional classicists will quickly show[97]—it is more likely that, if we let them, our students will look at the past with fresh, more objective eyes.

---

* Christian parents who are concerned about the study of classical cultures may wish to read Appendix B, "Classical Studies and the Christian: A Note to Parents."

97. See, for example, the blistering critiques by Victor Davis Hanson and John Heath in *Who Killed Homer?* (ISBN 1893554260) and *Bonfire of the Humanities* (ISBN 1882926544).

We simply cannot underestimate the influence of the ancients—especially the Greeks—on our lives. What have the Greeks given us? Look at nearly any academic discipline, from physics to philosophy to political science, and you will find the fingerprints of the Greeks. Their very language, along with Latin, forms the basis for the bulk of our English vocabulary. Therefore, to neglect the study of classical cultures is to neglect our own cultural patrimony. As the poet Shelley famously said, "We are all Greeks."

Curriculum Overview

	Primary School	Grammar School	Secondary School
Goals	Introduce young students to basic stories in the classical tradition	Gain familiarity with classical myth, history, biography, drama, and epic poetry	In-depth study of key examples of classical drama, poetics, and philosophy
Materials	Aesop's *Fables*; picture-book versions of Greek, Roman, and Norse myths	D'Aulaires' *Greek Myths* and *Famous Men of Rome* (Memoria Press courses); *Boys' and Girls' Plutarch*; *The Iliad*; *The Odyssey*; *The Aeneid*; *The Oresteia*	Greek dramatists (Sophocles, Euripides), Aristotle's *Poetics* and *Nicomachean Ethics*, Marcus Aurelius's *Mediations*, Plato's *Republic*

Classical Studies in the Primary-School Years (K-2)

Just as we provide a gentle introduction to the classical languages in these years, we approach classical cultures with equal simplicity. Students will benefit from Aesop's homely wisdom and will enjoy picture-book versions of the basic Greek, Roman, and Norse myths. Read these many times so that the stories become familiar to your child.

Reading Selections for Kindergarten

Aesop's Fables. These simple, enduring stories are the perfect entry into classical studies. Choose a generous, well-illustrated collection such as the affordable *Aesop for Children,* illustrated by Milo Winter (ISBN 0590479776).

Reading Selections for First Grade

Greco-Roman Myths. Your student will be spending much more time on Greek and Roman mythology in the grammar-school years. At this point, the goal is to introduce her to some of the basic stories. Begin the study of Greek mythology with Aliki's *Gods and Goddesses of Olympus* (ISBN 0064461890), which follows Hesiod's narrative faithfully, but in an age-appropriate way. Then choose a selection of picture books, such as *Pegasus* (ISBN 0688133827), *King Midas and the Golden Touch* (ISBN 0688131654), and *Cupid and Psyche* (ISBN 0688131638), all lavishly illustrated by Kinuko Y. Craft. For the Romans, try *Roman Myths,* retold by Geraldine McCaughrean (ISBN 0689838220). You may find that the illustrations are a bit cartoonish, but the book covers some key Roman stories not found elsewhere.

Reading Selections for Second Grade

Norse Myths. Although not "classical" in the Mediterranean sense, these stories are nearly as important as the Greek and Roman myths: They prepare your student for reading the great Old English tales like *Beowulf* as well as modern classics inspired by Norse myth, such as *Lord of the Rings.* There are fewer individual picture books for the Norse material, so the best choices here are *D'Aulaires' Norse Gods and Gi-*

ants (ISBN 159017125X) or Mary Pope Osborne's *Favorite Norse Myths* (ISBN 0590480472). Kevin Crossley-Holland's *Norse Myths* (ISBN 0394748468) is a particularly rich retelling but has few illustrations.

Classical Studies in the Grammar-School Years (3-8)

Now begins the real meat of the Classical Studies program. Your student will spend a full year immersed in the Greek myths, those essential classical stories. One year is devoted to Roman history, and another to Greco-Roman biography. In sixth and seventh grades, the English Studies curriculum is rolled together with Classical Studies as the student tackles the great epic poets, Homer and Virgil. The transitional eighth-grade year sees the student's first exposure to Greek drama.

Reading Selections for Third Grade

D'Aulaires' *Greek Myths*. Work through the Memoria Press course (formerly part of their *Introduction to Classical Studies* curriculum) to gain mastery of these essential stories.

Reading Selections for Fourth Grade

***Famous Men of Rome*.** Memoria Press's course will introduce your student to key figures in Roman history.

Reading Selections for Fifth Grade

The Boys' and Girls' Plutarch or ***Famous Men of Greece*.** Students devote this year to a further study of Greco-Roman biography, either with John S. White's version of Plutarch's *Lives* (check your library or download from digital.library.upenn.edu/webbin/gutbook/lookup?num=2484) or with *Famous Men of Greece*. The latter is available, with study helps, in a new edition from Memoria Press (memoriapress.com); the original text can also be found online at http://www.mainlesson.com.

Reading Selections for Sixth Grade

Homer: *The Iliad* (translation: Butler, *more readable;* **Lattimore,** *more challenging*) **and the *Odyssey* (trans. Fitzgerald).** These works are so important that they stand in for both Classical Studies and English literature for this year. (Many students will need additional preparation before beginning these works. If so, study Olivia Coolidge's **The Trojan War** in sixth grade and move each year forward, skipping Sophocles and Euripides scheduled for the ninth grade.)

Please see the section on "Teaching Literature in the Grammar Years" (p. 92) for more information on how to explore these exhilarating but challenging texts with your student. Since these poems were originally performed orally—sung or chanted, actually—you may be able to catch the flavor of Homer best by listening to the books on tape. Numerous readings are available; try to sample a few from your library system before buying. If you'd like to hear some scholarly attempts to reconstruct Homeric performance, visit the Homeric Singing site (www.oeaw.ac.at/kal/sh/). You may also want to watch some of the film adaptations of these perennial stories. Not all are equally thrilling or true to Homer's vision, but if you and your student enjoy "sword and sandal" movies, give them a try.

The ancients did not shy away from using handbooks to teach the classics, and neither should you. I recommend that you invest in Malcolm M. Willcock's *A Companion to the Iliad* (ISBN 0226898555), an immensely useful line-by-line commentary keyed to the Lattimore translation. For the Odyssey, there is *A Guide to The Odyssey : A Commentary on the English Translation of Robert Fitzgerald*, by Ralph Hexter (ISBN 0679728473). Finally, if you're wondering what the big deal is about Homer in the first place, read Eva Brann's *Homeric Moments* (ISBN 096767570).

Reading Selection for Seventh Grade

Virgil: *The Aeneid*. What Homer is to Greek, Virgil is to Latin. The *Aeneid*, which Virgil consciously modeled on Homer's classics, can be considered the literary self-image of the Roman Empire. The language, even in translation, is lovely, with unexpectedly evocative images springing up even in the midst of battle scenes. Your student will be reading Virgil in the original in eleventh grade, but for now enjoy the story for its grandeur and emotion.

Reading Selection for Eighth Grade

Aeschylus: *The Oresteia*. The Greeks invented drama as we know it, and Aeschylus is the first of the great Greek tragedians. *The Oresteia* is a trilogy of tragedies that picks up the story of one of the returning heroes of the Trojan War. Do read these plays aloud, or seek out a production if at all possible. The plays will no doubt spark much debate about ancient Greek views of honor, family, guilt, and redemption, particularly when discussed in conjunction with this year's Christian Studies readings. In keeping with the transitional nature of the eighth-grade curriculum, Greek drama forms a bridge between epic in the late-grammar years and philosophy in the secondary-school years.

Classical Studies in the Secondary-School Years (9-12)

Secondary-school students continue their study of ancient drama with the younger generation of tragedians. Aristotle's *Poetics* bridges drama and philosophy and also helps the student begin to think more critically about his reading. The remaining three years are taken up key texts of the great schools of classical philosophy. Representing the Lyceum, we have Aristotle; Marcus Aurelius speaks for the Stoa; and Plato, for the Academy.

Reading Selections for Ninth Grade

Sophocles: *The Theban Plays*; Euripides: *The Bacchantes*; Aristotle: *Poetics*. The student gains more understanding of Greek tragedy by reading the two remaining masters of the genre, Sophocles and Euripides. Again, the plays should be read aloud for maximum effect. Aristotle places these writers in context by providing the student with a structure for thinking about the dramatic forms. How does the view of tragedy in these plays compare to that found in the book of Job, which students read in Christian Studies this year?

Reading Selection for Tenth Grade

Aristotle: *Nicomachean Ethics*. Having read C. S. Lewis's *Abolition of Man* two years before, students will be well prepared to tackle Aristotle. Arguably the most elevated statement of classical thought on ethics, Aristotle's work is remarkable for its readability and its humanity. The extended meditation on friendship speaks particularly clearly to teenagers.

Reading Selection for Eleventh Grade

Marcus Aurelius: *Meditations.* From Aristotelian thought, we turn to a premier example of Stoicism, the Roman emperor Marcus Aurelius. These deeply personal notes to himself reflect both his philosophy and his emotional life. Look for the robust translation by David Hicks and C. Scot Hicks, *The Emperor's Handbook* (ISBN 0743233832). To place this work in its proper context, have your student read Pierre Hadot's *What Is Ancient Philosophy?* (ISBN 0674013735), which explains why it is a mistake to think of philosophy apart from action—a sentiment Marcus Aurelius would certainly have approved.

Reading Selection for Twelfth Grade

Plato: *The Republic.* Finally, we reach the longest and most influential of Plato's dialogues, *The Republic.* This extended meditation on the ideal society brings into focus all the most pressing questions philosophy seeks to answer. While few moderns would subscribe wholeheartedly to Plato's vision, it will be enlightening for your student to read about an ancient philosopher's vision of the ideal education. This will no doubt give you and your student a chance to reflect on the student's experience as he makes decisions about his future path.

IX. CHRISTIAN STUDIES

Veritas liberabit vos. —**The Vulgate (John 8:32b)***

ℰℐ

It has been said that Western culture is the fruit of the encounter between Athens and Jerusalem. In Classical Studies, we linger in Athens. In Christian Studies, we sojourn in Jerusalem before following the spread of the church across Europe and into the New World. This subject treats the ancient and medieval portions of history as well as literature, the Bible, and Christian theology. Along with Classical Studies and Modern Studies, it forms part of the world history curriculum. You will find that the readings here feed into your student's study of rhetoric and the *progymnasmata,* logic, and of course, Latin and Greek.**

Curriculum Overview

	Primary School	Grammar School	Secondary School
Goals	Introduce children to key Bible stories; begin memorizing verses and prayers (optional)	Survey the Old and New Testaments; translate Latin Vulgate passages and hymns; read examples of modern apologetics	In-depth study of key books of the Bible (including some in Greek) and selected Christian classics
Materials	Picture books and/or children's Bible, Scripture memory curriculum (optional), catechism (optional)	Christian Studies I-III; Lingua Angelica; Lingua Biblica; *The Abolition of Man, Mere Christianity.*	Bible, *Pilgrim's Progress* and/or *Imitation of Christ*

* "The truth shall free you."

** Secular and non-Christian parents who have concerns about how to teach this subject may wish to read Appendix C, "Approaches to Christian Studies for the Non-Christian Family."

Christian Studies in the Primary-School Years (K-2)

Just as you approach Classical Studies through key stories, so also will these years be a time of gentle read-alouds and simple memory work. If your church uses a catechism, begin it in kindergarten or first grade. Memorization of Bible verses may begin even before kindergarten.

Reading Selections for Kindergarten through Second Grade

Bible Stories. In kindergarten, you are offering a very simple introduction to Scripture. Select from the myriad picture books about the creation, Noah's ark, the Christmas and Easter stories, the 23rd Psalm, and the Lord's Prayer. In first grade, the focus is on the basic stories of the Hebrew Bible (Old Testament). Use a well-illustrated children's picture Bible, like *Tomie dePaola's Book of Bible Stories* (ISBN 0698119231). Supplement with picture books, such those by Brian Wildsmith (*Exodus, Joseph*). In second grade, read the New Testament stories in your children's Bible, focusing on the parables and miracles of Jesus. There are many wonderful picture books to augment these readings. Tomie dePaola has illustrated two books that are perfect for reading this year: *The Parables of Jesus* (ISBN 0823411966) and *The Miracles of Jesus* (ISBN 0823411966). You may also want to include some saints' lives. Again, dePaola has written many beautiful ones (Mary, Patrick, Francis, Christopher), as have other children's writers.

Recitation for Kindergarten through Second Grade

Children can begin memorizing simple prayers and Scripture verses in kindergarten or even earlier. There are many formal programs available (see, for example, the materials at www.scripturememory.com or www.childrendesiringgod.org/fv_index.html), or you can simply select a dozen or more simple verses for the child to memorize. Also consider singing hymns or Bible songs at home. Plan to spend five or ten minutes a day learning and reviewing verses, prayers, and hymns.

Christian Studies in the Grammar-School Years (3-8)

In these years students read through a generous selection of Bible narratives, translate Latin hymns and passages from the Vulgate (Latin Bible), and read two books by one of the twentieth century's greatest Christian apologists, C. S. Lewis. The goal is to increase the student's familiarity with the language and meaning of the Bible and the core beliefs of Christianity.

If you belong to a church that uses a catechism or stresses Scripture memory, these are the prime years for that work. Plan to spend ten to fifteen minutes a day learning and reviewing this material. Parents may also wish to encourage daily personal devotions, family worship, or other religious activities at home and through their local congregations. These will only serve to apply and reinforce what students are learning in Christian Studies.

Reading Selections for Third Grade through Fifth Grade

Christian Studies I-III (www.memoriapress.com). Use these study guides (expanded from *Introduction to Classical Studies*) at the rate of one volume per year as your student reads and studies the *Golden Children's Bible* or another Bible version of your choice. If you do choose to go with straight Scripture rather than a retelling, I strongly recommend the King James Version, for literary, not theological, reasons. Familiarity with the cadences of the KJV will aid in reading much of the later material in the English and Christian Studies curricula (Shakespeare, Bunyan). If you prefer a modern translation, the English Standard Version is a good choice, as it retains the dignified literary tone of the KJV without sacrificing accuracy. An ESV Children's Bible is available (ISBN 1581347472).

In deciding which Bible version to use, parents may want to be aware of one less-than-ideal aspect of the otherwise excellent *Golden Children's Bible*: The illustrations depict Jesus as blond and blue-eyed. If you do want to use the *Golden Children's Bible*—and it *is* a wonderful book, much loved in our own home—you may want to explain that that Bible does not tell us exactly what Jesus looked like, but that it is likely that he resembled other Jewish men of the Middle East.

Reading Selections for Sixth and Seventh Grades

During these two years, Christian Studies comes together with Latin Memoria Press' translation programs, **Lingua Angelica**. As your student will already be making progress in Henle at this point, they should find this text an interesting change of pace.

Reading Selections for Eighth Grade

C. S. Lewis: *The Abolition of Man* **and** *Mere Christianity.* Lewis was the twentieth century's most popular apologist, and the new millennium has not dimmed his fame in the least. *The Abolition of Man* is at once a treatise on education, a ringing refutation of relativism, and a meditation on general revelation and ethics. *Mere Christianity,* which was developed from a series of radio talks, is a readable and forthright presentation of the gospel. Lewis was an adult convert and a member of the Church of England, but as his title indicates, the book speaks to the common heritage of Christians everywhere. I especially recommend this book to parents who are not familiar with Christian beliefs or whose only exposure to them was in childhood. Not only will *Mere Christianity* help you understand the assumptions of your Christian neighbors, but it will also give you and your student insight into the worldview that permeates the medieval reading selections in English Studies.

For further integration of Latin and Christian Studies, keep translating in *Lingua Angelica* or, you may use Memoria Press' **Lingua Biblica**, or familiar passages from the Vulgate online at www.mythfolklore.net/bible/stories.htm.

Christian Studies in the Secondary-School Years (9-12)

Secondary-school students study key books of the Bible—at least one of which is read in the original Greek—as well as Christian classics in Latin and English. (Please see the secondary-school Latin section for details on the Latin-language readings.) I have recommended some study notes for the Greek readings, but parents may wish to seek out commentaries on the various books that reflect their denomination's teachings. Better yet, read more than one commentary, especially ones that shed light on church history, such as Luther's and Calvin's approaches to Romans.

Reading Selection for Ninth Grade

Bible: Job. Scholars believe Job may be the oldest book of the Bible, and it deals with one of the perennial dilemmas of human life: Why do bad things happen to good people? Job makes an excellent foil to the Greek tragedies read in Classical Studies this year, offering a biblical alternative to their explanation of human suffering.

Reading Selection for Tenth Grade

Bible: Isaiah. This prophetic book provides the backdrop for much of the action in the Gospels. Who was this Messiah that the Jewish people were longing for? What were the prophecies that he would fulfill? What vision of God's kingdom did Isaiah bequeath to his people? The glorious imagery and majestic language of the second half of the book also make this one of the literary highlights of the Old Testament.

Reading Selection for Eleventh Grade

Bible: The Gospel According to John. John's life of Jesus is arguably the most theologically rich gospel narrative. It is also an excellent study in Biblical Greek. If your student has been studying *koine* all along, she should be ready to tackle the whole book in the original, but even students who have only begun Greek in ninth grade will still find themselves well prepared to read selections from the text in Greek. The full Greek text, plus excellent translation and study notes, can be found online at www.btinternet.com/~MisPar/GNotes/john.htm .

Reading Selections for Twelfth Grade

Bible: Epistle to the Romans. Paul's letter to the fledgling church at Rome lays out the process of salvation, from justification to adoption to sanctification, while arguing for the unity of Jewish and Gentile believers. Although the Greek includes some challenges for the translator—much ink has been spilled over the proper interpretation of *telos nomou,* literally translated *the goal [or end] of the law*—your student can read certain selections from the book in the original language. The text and study notes are available at www.btinternet.com/~MisPar/GNotes/romans.htm.

John Bunyan: *Pilgrim's Progress* **or Thomas à Kempis:** *The Imitation of Christ.* These two classics have profoundly influenced Western Christendom. Bunyan's allegory is often cited as second only to the Bible in numbers in print and made its mark on New World theology.

I urge parents to have their children read Bunyan even if their family's theology is not in accord with his; the profound influence of his work on English literature cannot be underestimated. However, if you object strongly to Bunyan—he was no friend to the Roman Catholic Church—you may wish to substitute Thomas à Kempis's *The Imitation of Christ,* an inspiring and influential Christian classic in its own right. Better yet, read both!

These works provide insight into the development of Christian thought and therefore expand upon the ancient and medieval works being read in Latin in this same year.

X. MODERN STUDIES

Οὐδὲ γλύκιον ἧς πατρίδος. —**Homer***

ℰℌ

Modern Studies picks up the thread of world history where Christian Studies leaves off, in the early-modern period. In the primary and grammar years, the focus is on national history** and world geography; in secondary school, the historical net is cast more widely.

Curriculum Overview

	Primary School	Grammar School	Secondary School
Goals	Introduce young students to well-known stories from national history and to basic geographical concepts and information	Survey American history; master world geography facts	Detailed study of Anglo-American history
Materials	Picture books, map, globe, atlas, *Geography Songs* CD	Artner *Reader's Guide to American History*; *Everything You Need to Know about American History Homework*; historical novels	Winston Churchill's *History of the English-Speaking Peoples*

---

* "Nothing is sweeter than one's native land."

** The outline here is designed for readers in the United States. Canadian readers will naturally want to substitute appropriate material about their own national history. Please see Appendix D for some suggestions.

Modern Studies in the Primary-School Years (K-2)

In keeping with the overall theme of the primary years, we empha-size the *story* in history. Basic geography facts and concepts are also in-troduced with maps and a globe.

Reading Selections for Kindergarten

Modern Studies is best approached topically in kindergarten, us-ing the calendar year and national holidays as a guide. Select picture books from your local library that introduce the following stories and historical figures: Native American myths and legends; Leif Ericsson (*Leif the Lucky* by Ingri D'Aulaire); Christopher Columbus; the Thanks-giving story (Pilgrims, Squanto); Martin Luther King, Jr.; Washington and Lincoln (Presidents' Day); 4th of July (the D'Aulaires' *Star-Spangled Banner*). Feel free to include other holidays and also picture-book biog-raphies of famous Americans whom your student finds interesting and inspiring: inventors, explorers, scientists, pioneers, religious leaders, and so on. *Books to Build On* (ISBN 0385316402) is an excellent resource for history-related picture books.

Geography Skills for Kindergarten

Geography studies begin with simple map work. Let your child look at a globe, a map of the United States (preferably one that shows our northern and southern neighbors as well), and a map of the world. You may also want to invest in a good, up-to-date atlas. Place these where the student spends most of her time, so that the images will become familiar. By the end of kindergarten, students should be able to identify the con-tinents and oceans; find the United States, Canada, and Mexico on both a map and a globe; and find their home state on a map. They should also be able to give the name of their state and its capital city, their county, and their town; identify major local landmarks (hills or mountains, waterways); and point to the cardinal directions when standing in a familiar location, such as their home.

Recitation for Kindergarten

Begin listening to a collection of American patriotic and folk songs, such as "Wee Sing America." (www.weesing.com)This CD comes with a lyric book with some historical background on the songs and also includes some recitations from the Declaration of Independence, the Constitution, the Gettysburg Address, and other important documents and speeches. These will become recitation material in the years to come. Amy L. Cohn's book, *From Sea to Shining Sea,* is another useful resource for American songs. See the section on second-grade English Studies for more details.

Reading Selections for First Grade (Read Aloud)

D'Aulaires: *Leif the Lucky, Columbus, Pocahontas.* Students learn about key early figures in North American history with these beloved biographies.

Holling C. Holling: *Paddle-to-the-Sea; Sea Bird.* These delightful books introduce children to geography with engaging stories and illustrations.

Geography Skills for First Grade

By the end of the year, students should be able to identify the following: continents, oceans, equator, poles, tropics, major countries, and some states on both a map and globe. A formal curriculum is not necessary, but if you want one, consider the Evan-Moor Beginning Geography Series (www.evan-moor.com). Three inexpensive workbooks cover Continents and Oceans; Land Forms and Bodies of Water; and How to Use a Map.

Recitation for First Grade

This year, students learn the Pledge of Allegiance, the motto of your state (which may be in Latin!), and the song "America the Beautiful."

Reading Selections for Second Grade (Read Aloud)

D'Aulaires: *George Washington, Benjamin Franklin, Abraham Lincoln.* More delightful biographies from the D'Aulaires. You may want to supplement with other picture books about these key figures in American history.

Holling C. Holling: *Minn of the Mississippi, Tree in the Trail.* These books teach North American geography with fresh and engaging storylines. Be sure to follow the progress of the characters on a map.

Recitation for Second Grade

Using the *Geography Songs* CD from Audio Memory (www.audiomemory.com), students learn the major countries on each continent. They should also learn the first verse of "The Star-Spangled Banner."

Modern Studies in the Grammar-School Years (3-8)

In the grammar-school years, you will shift to a more systematic, chronological study of American history and U.S. and world geography. The curriculum follows the **Artner Reader's Guide to American History** (www.memoriapress.com), which relies heavily on historical fiction. Students memorize a few key dates and geography facts, which can be found in summary form in the Artner guide and in greater detail in *Everything You Need to Know about American History Homework* (ISBN 0590493639). Memoria Press sells this book bundled with the Artner guide, or you can buy it separately.

You may also want to use an elementary-age narrative history, either as family reading or as assigned independent reading. Here there are several possibilities. The first—and the option I recommend—is to use volumes III and IV of Susan Wise Bauer's *Story of the World,* available in book and audio formats. These books have the benefit of placing national history in a broader historical context. Hillyer's *Child's History of the World,* while much more compact than Bauer's books, will also give an engaging overview in the context of world history. Other options include Helene A. Guerber's *The Story of the Thirteen Colonies* and *The Story of the Great Republic,* recently reprinted by Nothing New Press (www.nothingnewpress.com), and H. E. Marshall's *This Country of Ours.* Marshall's text is available online at www.gutenberg.org/etext/3761 .

I strongly recommend that parents carefully pre-read history texts. Here more than almost anywhere in the curriculum, political assumptions are a deciding factor. A text that is perfectly reasonable to one family might be rejected by another as hopelessly biased, even offensive. Be aware, as well, that older texts may use language that was current at the time of writing but is no longer acceptable. Modern editions usually update language in such cases.

Formal studies in geography are completed in seventh grade. I recommend that, at the end of the transitional eighth grade year, the student read an analytical history study in preparation for more advanced work in the secondary-school years.

To achieve mastery of the material, use a combination of memory work, oral and written narration, and family discussions. Starting in sixth or seventh grade, the student can begin to answer more analytical questions about history material: What was the key constitutional issue that sparked the Civil War, and what was the position of each side? How did the Industrial Revolution affect American cities and immigration? What was the goal of the New Deal and to what extent did it succeed in the short and long term? Such questions can be tackled in the standard five-paragraph essay using the techniques learned in the *progymnasmata*.

Reading Selections for Third Grade

This year, work through Artner Units 1 & 2: Exploration and Settlement (c. 1000-1607) and The Colonial Period (1607-1775), selecting appropriate historical fiction from the lists in the guide. You will want to read through the Teacher's Guide section (especially page 15) of Artner for an explanation of the program and a description of how best to use it.

Geography Skills for Third Grade

Identify on a map the fifty states and their capitals, plus major North American rivers and mountain ranges.

Recitation for Third Grade

Recite the fifty states and their capitals, and the dates from the Artner Basic Fact Sheets for Units 1 & 2.

Reading Selections for Fourth Grade

This year brings us to the War of Independence and the establishment of the United States government. Use Artner Unit 3: The War of Independence and the New Government (1775-1789).

Geography Skills for Fourth Grade

Identify North and South American countries, rivers, and mountains on a map and a globe. Have your student read some library books on the various countries you're studying this year, especially our nearest neighbors, Canada and Mexico. For some possible readings in Canadian history and geography, see Appendix D.

Recitation for Fourth Grade

Recite the presidents in order as well as the dates from the Artner Basic Fact Sheets for Unit 3.

Reading Selections for Fifth Grade

This year, you will work through Artner Unit 4: National Development and Westward Expansion (1790-1877) with your student. (Some of this material will be covered in greater depth in sixth grade, hence the overlap in dates.)

Geography Skills for Fifth Grade

Identify countries, mountains, and rivers of Europe. Check out library books on the various countries for independent reading.

Recitation for Fifth Grade

Recite the Preamble to the Constitution and the dates from the Artner Basic Fact Sheets for Unit 4.

Reading Selections for Sixth Grade

This year brings us to a particularly difficult chapter in American history, covered in Artner Unit 5: Civil War and Reconstruction (1861-1877).

Geography Skills for Sixth Grade

Identify the countries, mountains, and rivers of Asia and Australia. Again, include a few books about these countries as part of your student's independent reading.

Recitation for Sixth Grade

Recite the introduction to the Gettysburg Address and the dates from the Artner Basic Fact Sheets for Unit 5.

Reading Selections for Seventh Grade

Artner Unit 6: Industrial Revolution and the Rise of American World Leadership (1878-1918) is the focus of this year's studies.

Geography Skills for Seventh Grade

In this final year of formal geography studies, students identify the countries, mountains, and rivers of Africa and read books about some of the major African nations.

Recitation for Seventh Grade

Recite the Bill of Rights and the dates from the Artner Basic Fact Sheets for Unit 6.

Reading Selections for Eighth Grade

This year sees the student cover two units on twentieth-century America: Artner Units 7 & 8: Boom, Depression and WWII (1919-1945) and The American Century (1946-present).

In addition, I recommend that students spend at least a quarter of the year, if not a full semester, reading and discussing Russell Kirk's **The Roots of American Order.** This excellent study places American history in the context not just of the classical heritage, but of the British common-law system. It provides excellent preparation for the Modern Studies readings from Churchill in the secondary-school years. Readers who are not familiar with Kirk should be aware that his perspective is an emphatically conservative one. I do not know of any text that would make a suitable alternative, however.

Recitation for Eighth Grade

Recite the dates from the Artner Basic Fact Sheets for Units 7 and 8 and list the amendments to the US Constitution.

Modern Studies in the Secondary-School Years (9-12)

Here the student begins an in-depth study of Anglo-American history in the context of broader world historical events. The recommended text is Winston Churchill's four-volume *History of the English-Speaking Peoples,* read at the rate of one volume per school year. The set has recently been reprinted by the Akadine Press (www.commonreader.com); older editions are readily found on the used market. A single-volume condensed version is also available; while it would not provide sufficient material for four years' study, it might be of use to parents who want to limit Modern Studies to two years in high school.

Students should be expected to write regular essays that demonstrate their understanding of the topics addressed in Churchill. It is desirable that the assigned essay topics require the students to integrate their knowledge of ancient and medieval history with Modern Studies.

Reading Selections for Ninth through Twelfth Grades

Read one volume of Churchill's text per year. The first volume covers British history from 55 B.C. to A.D. 1485. The second volume shifts to the New World. The third looks at the age of revolution, and the final volume as the Anglo-American democratic tradition.

Recitation for Ninth through Twelfth Grades

The English Studies curriculum for these years calls for practice in oratory using speeches from plays and from history. You can integrate selections relevant to your history reading into oratory. In ninth grade, for example, the student might learn Antony's famous speech from "Julius Caesar" as he reads about the Roman conquest of Britain in Churchill. The final year would suggest some of the great speeches of the twentieth century, including Churchill's own.

XI. SCIENCE

Εὕρηκα! (*Eureka!*) —**Archimedes**

ೞ

In the ancient world, the natural sciences were a branch of philosophy. Unfortunately, today science is often set in opposition to the humanities, "hard facts" against fuzzy, non-quantifiable ideals. Such a view divorces the sciences from the intellectual matrix that ultimately gives them meaning.

What's more, science is not like Latin grammar, a static body of knowledge that one can master in a few years of hard work. Rather, it is like history—constantly changing, constantly expanding. As new theories and discoveries shape our view of the natural world, the content of science as a discipline changes, too.

Finally, it should be noted that science—particularly laboratory-based experimental science—was not commonly taught as part of the traditional classical curriculum. In fact, those who study the history of science have commented on how many early scientists were amateurs whose discoveries grew out of what we might best describe as passionately pursued hobbies.

All this makes it challenging to propose a classical approach to science that stays true to the philosophical roots of the discipline while taking into consideration the very real needs of today's students. It should therefore be understood that what I suggest here is, in one sense, the least "traditional" of all the subjects discussed so far. I do believe, however, that it is true to the spirit of both ancient and modern scientific inquiry and that it avoids the common pitfalls of irrelevance and tedium.

What I propose is an approach that aims at achieving scientific literacy—the ability to understand and make informed judgment about scientific matters. Instead of focusing on the frontiers of science or on controversial topics, students spend their time mastering the basics through first-hand observation and careful reading.

In the early years, these basics consist of facts and ideas about the natural world: why the seasons change, what sort of societies insects form, how the Grand Canyon came to be. Later, the student will systematize this knowledge as she gains understanding of the assumptions, processes, and laws of each major branch of science. Finally, reading widely on topics of personal interest, the student will seek to form judgments about the meaning of the scientific knowledge she has acquired: What opinion might a citizen form about the funding of this or that research project? To what uses may technology be rightly put? How does this or that theory or discovery help humans live what the ancient philosophers called the good life?

Throughout the science curriculum, the following elements should be emphasized:

(1) the history of science, including biographies of famous scientists;

(2) the scope of each of the major fields of science, and their key assumptions, milestones, laws, and processes;

(3) concern for how the sciences relate to other fields, such as economics, politics, and philosophy.

Curriculum Overview

	Primary and Grammar Years	Secondary Years
Goals	Delight-based exploration of the natural world; survey of the various scientific disciplines (8th grade)	Scientific literacy and the ability to view science in relationship to the humanities
Materials	Library books and field guides, museums, nature walks; *Science Matters* (8th grade)	Selected readings from scientific journals, books, and other research materials; reference works and study guides

Science in the Primary-School Years (K-2)

During the primary years, students study nature informally with regular nature walks, picture books, and field trips to science museums, zoos, botanical gardens, and the like. At this age, scientific learning should be both practical (seasons, planets, calendar, domestic and farm animals) and delight-based (dinosaurs, horses, star-gazing, rock-collecting, bird-watching).

Science in the Grammar-School Years (3-8)

Science continues to be pursued informally from grades three through seven. This is the time to introduce biographies of famous scientists. Your public library's science section will be your curriculum guide during these years, as will natural events (meteor showers and eclipses, cicada cycles, local planting and harvest times, bird or butterfly migrations) and local resources (zoos, state and national parks, nature preserves, science and natural history museums). The following topics can provide focus points in the grammar years:

- local wildlife and habitats;
- local growing season (plant a container garden; visit a farm);
- weather patterns (measure rainfall and temperature; observe cloud formations)
- animal life cycles (tadpoles, butterflies);
- insect societies (bees, ants);
- birds;
- trees and flowers;
- constellations and the solar system;
- rocks and minerals.

Consider investing in a substantial children's science encyclopedia, a selection of regional field guides, and perhaps binoculars, a microscope, or a telescope, depending on your student's interests. *Everything You Need to Know about Science Homework* (ISBN 0439625440) and *The New How Things Work* (ISBN 079226956X) are two additional reference guides to have on hand. Borrow volumes in the DK Eyewitness series and other topical studies from your library. If you prefer to follow a set schedule for science topics, refer to The Core Knowledge Series (*What Your ...Grader Needs to Know*), which contains excellent ideas for exploring science in the elementary grades.

In the transitional eighth grade year, the student reads **Science Matters,** by Hazen and Trefil (ISBN 038526108X) with the goal of achieving what the book's authors call "scientific literacy." This challenging book surveys the major fields of science, explains their assumptions and key findings, and ties all of this to contemporary concerns. I strongly recommend that the parent-teacher read this book in advance of, or alongside, the student.* Although *Science Matters* is written for a general audience, not for specialists, it is an adult book, and some of the material may prove difficult. Parents should not hesitate to supplement this year's reading as needed with encyclopedias; popular introductions, like the *For Dummies* series; or test-prep and review materials, like the Barron's or Kaplan's AP or SAT II books.

The student should take careful notes and write a two-to-three page summary of the main points of each chapter, including any scientific assumptions, laws, or milestones mentioned. This information can be used as a starting point for further reading, or, in the secondary-school years, for research.

---

* The chapter on evolution is dismissive of young-earth creationism and doesn't address positions like theistic evolution or intelligent design. Christian parents with concerns about these issues may wish to discuss this chapter with their students and perhaps provide additional reading material.

Science in the Secondary-School Years (9-12)

Having reached the secondary-school years, the student is now adequately prepared for the kind of rigorous analysis that science requires. By this time, the habit of attention to detail, gained through the study of classical languages and arithmetic, is well ingrained and can be successfully applied to scientific knowledge.

Instead of learning about science by means of the usual mixture of textbooks and experiment kits, I suggest that the student immerse herself in specific topics of personal interest—something akin to the all-consuming "hobbies" of the great amateur scientists of the past. This method is in keeping with the *multum non multa* principle: Rather than attempting a whirlwind survey of a mass of scientific information—the usual textbook approach—the student explores a few key topics in depth and with reference to the rest of the classical curriculum. In the process, he does learn key facts, but these details are embedded in a context that makes them meaningful and allows the student to form judgments about their use and value.

How does this approach work? Taking her cues from the material in *Science Matters,* the student chooses two topics per year to research. One topic should involve direct collection of data by observation or experiment; the other, the reading and assessment of studies conducted by others. Research materials will include seminal historical works ("Great Books") as well as more recent articles and studies, and should tie the subject to larger, philosophical concerns, such as ethics. The results of these inquiries are written up in the form of a research paper or lab report.

I suggest a minimum of two years' science study in secondary school. During that time, the student should complete at least one project in each of the major fields: earth science, biology, chemistry, and physics. Students with a special interest in science and those who plan to apply to selective colleges may wish to continue for an additional one or two years along these lines, expanding the number of fields explored to include astronomy, environmental science, and technology.

While I believe that a course like the one described here, unconventional as it may seem at first glance, will be more than adequate preparation for further study, parents and students should certainly take into consideration college plans when deciding how to approach science in these years. Potential science majors who plan to apply to highly selective schools may be better served by a more conventional sequence of science courses—Earth Science, Biology, Chemistry, and Physics—using the *Essentials of...* series from Singapore Science or a similar curriculum. Lab-based courses might best be pursued in a co-op, cottage school, or community college setting to allow safe and ready access to specialized equipment. Whatever the case, every effort should be made to include both the history and ethics of science in these studies. At no time should science be presented as entirely separate from other fields of human endeavor.

The goal of this approach to science is to familiarize students not just with scientific facts—as important as these are—but also with scientific methods. This approach teaches students about the real work of contemporary scientists and harkens back to the observations of ancient scientific pioneers like Archimedes and Aristotle.

For Parents:

Science for All Americans (ISBN 0195067711, and free online at (wwwproject2061.org/tools/sfaaol/sfaatoc.htm). Informative book that covers basic premises of science, associated skills, and the habits of mind that characterize and support scientific inquiry. Although you may not agree with all the assumptions voiced in this book, it will give you insight into the nature of contemporary science, along with recommendations from scientists on how to teach the subject.

Reading Selections for Ninth and Tenth Grade

During these two years, the student undertakes a course of topical reading in a few scientific disciplines of his choice. The reading selections should include the history of the discipline along with biographies of prominent scientists in the field; material that discusses the field's key assumptions, milestones, laws, and processes; and an examination of the relationship of the field to other disciplines, such as ethics or politics. Each study culminates in a research paper, lab report, or other project, with appropriate documentation, that demonstrates the student's knowledge of the field.

Possible areas of study include, but are not limited to: astronomy, biology, botany, zoology (or any of its sub-fields, such as ornithology or entomology), chemistry, robotics, physics, earth science, meteorology, genetics, computer science, and medicine.

Because of the wide range of possible topics, I cannot give specific book recommendations. Instead, I offer the following reading and research program to help your student narrow down her area of interest and search out appropriate research material.

(1) Re-read the section in *Science Matters* on the general area of science to be studied, noting the key assumptions, milestones, laws, and processes mentioned. Note also areas of current research.

(2) Read one or more substantial encyclopedia articles on the subject, following up on the items mentioned in *Science Matters.*

(3) Beginning with the "Additional Reading" suggestions in *Science Matters,* read a general history of the field, noting major periods of development and milestones.

(4) Read at least one biography of a scientist who has made major innovations in the field.

(5) Collect and read articles from scientific journals or popular science magazines, and books, dealing with a particular aspect of the field that interests you.

(6) Search out articles that deal with the ethical or political implications of your area of interest.

(7) Based on your reading, develop a question to address in your research paper or a hypothesis to be tested.

(8) Read relevant studies or test your hypothesis by observation or experiment.

(9) Write the research paper or lab report, demonstrating your mastery of the material.

For example, a ninth-grade student with an interest in zoology might decide to make a special study of the Eastern lowland gorilla for his biology project. He would read about primate biology; poaching and the bush-meat trade; the political climate in the Democratic Republic of the Congo; the life and work of Dian Fossey; conditions in the Kahuzi-Biega National Park, etc. He might borrow videos from the library, conduct Internet research, or read interviews with researchers in the field. At this stage, he decides to write about threats to native gorilla habitats and the efforts of zoos to save and breed the animals. The student might visit a zoo to observe gorillas in captivity and interview a keeper. The final research paper could incorporate information from his historical and biographical readings, facts on gorilla habitats and family groupings, statistics on gorilla populations, a discussion of political and economic factors affecting preservation and breeding efforts, and, finally, his own assessment of the situation and suggestions for possible solutions.

In a second project in the same year, the student decides to study the effects of soil pH on tomato crop yield. This project would involve hands-on experiments with the plants as well as reading about plant structures, soil chemistry, and the like. The student might build models of certain molecules that appear in the soil (nitrogen, for example), or analyze the pH of various types of compost. To get ideas for projects and to learn about ways to organize and present findings, the student may want to consult one of the many books on science fair projects. Reference books and subject outlines may also come in handy.

XII. LOGIC

❧

It has been said that critical-thinking skills are a natural result of a classical education, and this opinion is not unfounded. Still, generations of educators have lauded the formal study of logic as an independent discipline. I recommend a series of courses by Martin Cothran in traditional and material logic bridging the late-grammar and early secondary-school years (seventh-tenth grades). Eleventh and twelfth graders may pursue additional logic study, choosing which direction to take based on their interests and other commitments.

Curriculum Overview

	Grammar School	Secondary School
Goals	To master the basics of traditional logic in the late grammar years.	To master a course in Material Logic and Logical Fallacies, and, optionally, to apply logical principles to philosophy and/or theology
Materials	*Traditional Logic I & II*	*Material Logic I*; *The Fallacy Detective*; *Rulebook for Arguments*; Kreeft's *Socratic Logic* and *Great Dialogues of Plato* (optional)

Logic in the Grammar-School Years (7-8)

In the grammar-school years, students become familiar with traditional logic. This language-based approach is preferable to symbolic logic at this stage.

Curriculum for Seventh and Eighth Grade

Work through Martin Cothran's **Traditional Logic** texts (www.memoriapress.com), using Book I in seventh grade and Book II in eighth. These books approach the subject systematically, with plenty of clear explanations and useful exercises. Instructional videos and DVDs are available for both volumes of *Traditional Logic*.

Logic in the Secondary-School Years

In the upper grades, students complete the Memoria Press logic sequence and then study logical fallacies and debate. If desired, they can continue with logic and classical philosophy in eleventh and twelfth grade.

Curriculum for Ninth and Tenth Grade

In ninth grade, use Martin Cothran's **Material Logic I**. A second volume is expected along with a course in fallacies, but at this writing no publication date has been announced. Therefore, I would suggest that you devote tenth grade to a special study of logical fallacies and debate. For this, your student can work through **The Fallacy Detective,** a 36-lesson curriculum by Nathaniel Bluedorn and Hans Bluedorn (www.triviumpursuit.com). Use Anthony Weston's **A Rulebook for Arguments** as a reference.

Curriculum for Eleventh Grade and Twelfth Grade

At this stage, your student will have a good grounding in logic, and so may opt not to continue formal study of the subject. If you do want your student to go on in logic, my recommendation is combine a close reading of selections from **Great Dialogues of Plato** (ISBN 0451527453) with a further course in classical logic: **Socratic Logic: A Logic Text Using Socratic Method, Platonic Questions, and Aristotelian Principles** by Peter Kreeft. Kreeft is a brilliant and engaging writer; you could not ask for a better guide to logic at this stage. Christian students may also wish to read his excellent *Handbook of Christian Apologetics,* co-authored by Ronald K. Tacelli (ISBN 0830817743).

XIII. AND THE REST:
MODERN LANGUAGES AND THE ARTS

Man soll alle Tage wenigstens ein kleines Lied hören, ein gutes Gedicht lesen, ein treffliches Gemälde sehen und, wenn es möglich zu machen wäre, einige vernünftige Worte sprechen. —**Johann Wolfgang von Goethe***

ℰ⌁

Modern Languages

You may find it strange that someone who holds a doctorate in a modern language (German), and who has taught that language to students from age six to age seventy-six, would relegate non-classical foreign languages to the unglamorous category of "other" and tell you not to worry about them until secondary school or even college. But that's exactly what I'm doing. Why?

There are two reasons. First, there are only so many hours in the day. It is all too easy, having pared down the curriculum to a few key disciplines, to fill it back up again with subjects of secondary importance. Remember Valerie Bendt's words of wisdom: "We should not allow the good things to crowd out the best things." Having studied six languages beyond the beginning level and several more to the "informed tourist" level, I can tell you that no modern European language exercises the mind as do Latin and Greek.

Second, Latin and Greek are the best training for the modern languages, just as they are for English. Students who have mastered Latin will pick up Romance languages such as French and Spanish with ease, since they typically draw eighty percent or more of their vocabulary from Latin. Nor are the classical languages useful preparation only for Latinate languages: Students will find that their experience with Latin

---

* "Every day one should at least try to hear a little song, read a good poem, view an excellent painting, and, if at all possible, speak a few reasonable words."

and Greek will serve them well in learning other inflected languages, such as German and Russian, and, of course, modern Greek.

There are some circumstances in which spending time on a modern language in the primary and grammar grades makes sense. Bilingual families, families living abroad, and those in bilingual or multilingual environments: all of these will have good reasons to teach a second (or third) language in childhood.

If you do choose to introduce your child to a modern foreign language, I urge you to begin as early as possible, ideally in infancy. Although such studies will add time and effort to the curriculum in the grammar-school years, an early start has significant advantages in terms of the child's developing accent in the target language.

You know that you don't need to worry over-much about your children's accent in Latin—no native speakers are likely to pop up to correct them. Conversely, you don't need to put too much emphasis on formal grammar in a modern language until the student has mastered the core vocabulary and a set of common phrases. (Of course, if at some point your student will be attending a school in which the target language is also the teaching language, your fluency goals will be different.) In other words, teach the modern language just as you taught English: Speak it to the child, read it to the child, sing songs, play games, encourage the child to repeat common words and phrases, and praise to the skies each baby step along the road to oral fluency. If you yourself are not a native speaker of the target language, do try to expose the child to authentic and fluent speech early and often. This might take the form of a friend or relative, an audio tape, a television show or video, radio or Internet programs, a babysitter, or a tutor hired specifically to come speak the language to and with your child for half an hour a week. For suggestions on how to approach foreign language study with a grammar-age child, I highly recommend Opal Dunn's book *Help Your Child with a Foreign Language* from the Berlitz Kids series (ISBN 2831568064). It is packed with concrete teaching ideas, including scripts for the first few lessons, and is home school-friendly.

Once the child has reached the late grammar-school years or secondary school, you may introduce a formal curriculum that covers grammar and uses a more systematic approach to vocabulary-building. It is vital that the student have a chance to practice their speaking skills in a group setting, especially with native speakers. I therefore recommend that you consider a home school co-op or community college class if at all possible, or hire a tutor to practice conversation skills.

The Arts

One of the criticisms leveled at classical and neoclassical education is that they give short shrift to the fine and performing arts, and yet we have seen that at least some ancient educators believed strongly in the formative powers of music. Further, the emphasis on classical cultures alongside classical languages necessarily includes the arts.

One of the great benefits of the pared-down classical curriculum is that it allows ample time for students to pursue personal interests, and primary among these are the arts. Music or dance lessons, drawing or photography classes, drama clubs: all these are available to your students, and I urge you to make them a part of your student's education. In fact, I suggest that you set music alongside Latin and math as one of the "daily disciplines" of your home school.

Children should, from an early age, be exposed not only to great literature, but to great art and great music as well. By this I do not mean a selection of Mozart claiming to increase the child's IQ, but simply the best examples of a variety of musical styles. It is not necessary to sit the child down and make them listen intently to such music; in fact, I would suggest that, at least in the earliest years, it is more effective to treat music as a backdrop for daily activities. As Shinichi Suzuki showed, children naturally learn music the same way that they learn to speak their native language: through repeated listening and imitation. Likewise, a child who is used to seeing high-quality paintings or art prints and beautifully illustrated picture books will be well prepared for the formal study of art later on. In the grammar-school years, for example, music and art appreciation can easily be integrated into the history curriculum. Charlotte Mason's method of "Picture Study" is one way to help children become familiar with the great artists and their works.*

Think of studio art and the study of an instrument (or voice), drama, or dance as in the same category as independent and family reading. Although not part of formal lesson time, they are a vital part of a rich liberal education, and without them, the classical curriculum would be impoverished; indeed, it would be incomplete.

---

* For a concise summary of this method, see Penny Gardner's description at www.digis.net/ ~gardnerp/art.html and for a possible schedule, the Ambleside Online site: www.amblesideonline. org/ArtSch.shtml .

APPENDIX A

Suggestions for Independent and Family Reading

These suggestions complement the main reading selections in English Studies, Modern Studies, Classical Studies, or Christian Studies. Books marked with an asterisk are highly recommended as supplements to the main selections. This is, however, by no means a comprehensive list of all the books you might want to assign or read with your child.

Kindergarten

A Child's Garden of Verses by Robert Louis Stevenson (various editions)
The Complete Tales of Winnie-the-Pooh by A. A. Milne (ISBN 0525457232)
The Complete Tales of Beatrix Potter (ISBN 0723247609)

First Grade

Egyptian Myths by Jacqueline Morley (ISBN 0872265897)
Red Fairy Book, Blue Fairy Book, etc. by Andrew Lang (available from Dover Publications)

Second Grade

Druids, Gods & Heroes from Celtic Mythology by Anne Ross (ISBN 0872269191)
Tales from the Mabinogion by Gwyn Thomas & Kevin Crossley-Holland (ISBN 0879516372)

Third Grade

Our Young Folks' Josephus by William Shepherd (ISBN 0974990000)
*Story of the World, vol.1, by Susan Wise Bauer (ISBN 0971412901)
The Chronicles of Narnia, by C. S. Lewis (seven-volume series, can be read over several years)
Calliope and Cobblestone (these magazines can be used throughout the grammar years)

Fourth Grade

Boys' and Girls' Herodotus (www.veritaspress.com)
*Story of the World, vol.1, by Susan Wise Bauer (ISBN 0971412901)
Cleopatra by Diane Stanley (ISBN 0688154808)
Good Queen Bess: The Story of Elizabeth I of England by Diane Stanley (ISBN 0688179614)
*Bard of Avon: The Story of William Shakespeare by Diane Stanley (ISBN 0688162940)

Fifth Grade

Favorite Medieval Tales by Mary Pope Osborne (ISBN 0439141346)
Famous Men of the Middle Ages by John Haaren (ISBN 188251405X)
An Island Story by H. E. Marshall (digital.library.upenn.edu/women/marshall/england/england.html)
*Story of the World, vol. 2 by Susan Wise Bauer (ISBN 0971412936)
Joan of Arc by Diane Stanley (ISBN 0064437485)

Sixth Grade

Famous Men of Greece by John Haaren (ISBN 1882514017)
*Theogony and Works and Days by Hesiod (various editions)
Homeric Hymns (various editions)
*Story of the World, vol. 3 by Susan Wise Bauer (ISBN 0971412995)

Seventh Grade

* Augustus Caesar's World by Genevieve Foster (ISBN 0964380323)
Metamorphoses by Ovid (various editions)
*Story of the World, vol. 4 by Susan Wise Bauer (ISBN 0972860339)

Eighth Grade

God in the Dock: Essays on Theology and Ethics by C. S. Lewis (ISBN 0802808689)
The Bible (to be read in its entirety over a period of months or years)

Ninth Grade

Histories by Herodotus (various editions)
"Against Cataline" by Cicero (various editions)
*The Birds (and other plays) by Aristophanes (various editions)
Till We Have Faces: A Myth Retold by C. S. Lewis (ISBN 0156904365)

Tenth Grade

Anabasis, Conversations of Socrates, and A History of My Times by Xenophon (various editions)

* *The Landmark Thucydides: A Comprehensive Guide to the Peloponnesian War* by Robert B. Strassler (ISBN 0684827905)

Francis and Clare: The Complete Works (ISBN 0809124467)

How to Speak, How to Listen by Mortimer Adler (ISBN 0684846470)

Eleventh Grade

The Early History of Rome by Livy (various editions)

The Annals of Imperial Rome, The Agricola, and *The Germanica* by Tacitus (various editions)

*Letters from a Stoic by Seneca (various editions)

Twelfth Grade

The Twelve Caesars by Suetonius (various editions)

The Ecclesiastical History of the English People by the Venerable Bede (various editions)

*Augustine of Hippo: Selected Writings (ISBN 0809125730)

The Odes by Pindar (various editions)

Odes and Epodes by Horace (various editions)

*Dialogues by Plato (various selections and editions)

Romantic Poetry and Prose, ed. H. Bloom and L. Trilling (ISBN 0195016157)

The Space Trilogy: Out of the Silent Planet (ISBN 0743234901) *Perelandra* (ISBN 074323491X), and *That Hideous Strength* (ISBN 0743234928) by C. S. Lewis

The Screwtape Letters by C. S. Lewis (ISBN 0060652934)

APPENDIX B

Classical Studies and the Christian: A Note to Parents

In the past decade, as classical education has moved to the forefront of the home schooling movement, we have seen serious debates about the proper place of Greek and Roman cultural studies in the curriculum. Some Christians have an understandable ambivalence toward "the pagans," and as we have seen, this is nothing new. The Church Fathers struggled with the same issues we moderns do, although they did not always come to the same conclusions. Is it true that an unbound focus on classical Greek and Roman literature would drive us in every direction except toward Christ"?[98] Is it accurate to claim, as one Christian curriculum publisher does, that the "classical Greek approach focuses on Greek literature and man's reasoning. The Hebrew methods focus on God's Word and faith"?[99]

Generations of classically educated Christians have shown these objections to be overstated, and anyone who has ever attended or visited a yeshiva (institution for Torah study and the study of Talmud) will know that "man's reasoning" is far from absent there. We have not seen mass apostasy among Christians as the result of reading a little Ovid. In fact, the generations of Christians who most valued classical education—including the Puritans and the more recent cohort that included Tolkien, Lewis, and Sayers—have been among the most devout and skilled apologists.

I assume that Christian parents will want do all they can to establish and encourage their children in the faith, and education is, obviously, central to that endeavor. Yes, it is possible to pursue a classical education without becoming, or remaining, a Christian. But as parents have discovered too late, it is also possible to attend Christian schools for twelve years and emerge a right heathen. It is not this or that curriculum that makes us people of faith; it is God's Spirit moving in us.

98. Bluedorns, p. 29.

99. www.homeschoolinformation.com/Approaches/classical.htm . Viewed 5/31/05.

We should not confuse general revelation with divine revelation, nor reject the former because we have the latter.[100] Nor should we dismiss what is good and beautiful and true in the created world because we have been given a glimpse the Good, the Beautiful, and the True in eternity. Human reason is a gift of God, and like all gifts, it is to be used in his service and to his glory. It is my hope and my prayer that your child's experience with Classical Studies, as with the entire classical curriculum, will equip him to exercise his God-given gifts rightly and joyfully.

---

100. cf. Cheryl Lowe, "Why Study the Pagans?" www.memoriapress.com/articles/whypagans.html . Viewed 5/31/05.

APPENDIX C

Approaches to Christian Studies for the Non-Christian Family

Before I became a Christian, I found myself frustrated by the fact that the classical curriculum was so often presented as the exclusive domain of Christianity. How could this be, I asked myself, when the foundations of classical education were well established before the birth of Jesus?

I have tried, in writing this book, not to assume that my readers share my faith; indeed, some of the people who gave me the most encouragement during the writing process are secular or members of other faiths. I want this book to be useful to them as well as to my Christian brothers and sisters.

That being the case, it may seem hypocritical of me to include an entire subject called "Christian Studies," complete with Scripture memory suggestions and references to "your church." How is the non-Christian parent to approach such a thing?

Just as I assume that Christian parents will teach stories from the Bible as religious truth, I assume that non-Christian parents will not. I also assume that members of other faiths will be just as diligently conveying their beliefs and values to their children as Christians are. That is part of our common responsibility as parents.

As classical home schoolers, we must all recognize the cultural value of the Bible even if we disagree on its formative value or normative authority in our lives. Even if the Bible does not hold pride of place in your worldview, I urge you to strive to give your children the gift of biblical literacy. Unless your student is familiar with these stories, it will be difficult, if not impossible, for her to understand many of the Great Books and other monuments of Western culture. For more information on how to approach the Bible as an academic study, please visit the Bible Literacy Project (www.biblecurriculum.org/Site/).

Please feel free to adapt the Christian Studies curriculum to meet your family's needs. It is certainly possible to study the suggested Bible books and Christian writings as literature. Members of other religions can substitute material from their faith traditions for the Christian recitation suggestions, and secular families may wish to use poetry or other material that they find inspiring and expressive of their highest values.

While I do believe that classical education is consonant with Christian teaching and that the tradition now includes a great deal of Christian material, I see no reason for non-Christian families to reject classical education as "not for us." Classical education represents our common heritage, and I hope that you will claim it as your own.

APPENDIX D

Modern Studies Selections for Canadian Readers

Canadian readers will need to substitute appropriate resources in their own national history for the US-focused curricula suggested in Modern Studies chapter. Here are a few ideas culled from Canadian classical educators. Most can be purchased from the Home Works catalogue (www.thehomeworks.ca). In the secondary-school years, students can use Churchill, which covers North American history in the context of our shared British heritage.

Reading Selections for the Primary-School Years (K-2)

My First History of Canada by Donalda Dickie (ISBN 096810231X). A good first introduction to Canadian history to read aloud.

Reading Selections the Grammar-School Years (3-8)

Courage and Conquest by Donna Ward. This worktext hits the major moments in Canadian history and includes workbook pages. Its greatest strength is the "top resources" list that will allow you to put together a reading program in Canadian history that parallels the approach of the *Artner Reader's Guide.*

For geography, you can use **The Big Book of Canada** by Christopher Moore (ISBN 0887764576), a beautifully illustrated volume that explores the provinces and territories as well as key events and figures in Canadian history.

Older students may enjoy **Canada, A People's History**, a mini-series from CBC Television. The videos and accompanying books should be available at your local library, or may be purchased from the CBC Web site: history.cbc.ca/histicons/ .

RESOURCES

Visit www.LatinCentered.com for direct links to resources mentioned in this book. Please post your comments or contact the author through our forums and blog.

American Classical League
Miami University
Oxford, OH 45056
513-529-7741
www.aclclassics.org
    Resources for the study of Latin and Greek

Bolchazy-Carducci Publishers, Inc.
1000 Brown Street, Unit 101
Wauconda IL 60084
800-392-6453
www.bolchazy.com
    Artes Latinae program; other Latin and Greek resources.

Canon Press and Book Service
P.O. Box 8729
Moscow ID 83843
800-488-2034
www.canonpress.org
    Logic texts and other classical resources.

Classical Composition
www.classicalcomposition.com
    English Composition curriculum and resources.

Classical Writing Store
www.lulu.com/classicalwriting
    The Classical Writing Series and other resources

Committee for the Promotion of Latin
www.camws.org
    Clearinghouse for information and materials for the study of Latin.

Henle Latin study group
groups.yahoo.com/group/HenleLatin

Highlands Latin School
Louisville KY
502-379-4057
www.thelatinschool.org

Intercollegiate Studies Institute (ISI)
P.O. Box 4431
Wilmington DE 19807
800-526-7022
http://www.isi.org
    Books and journals

Memoria Press
4105 Bishop Lane
Louisville KY 40218
502-966-9115
www.memoriapress.com
    Cheryl Lowe, *Classical Teacher*, resources for classical education,
    Latin, and language arts

Mythology-Folklore (Laura Gibbs' website)
www.mythfolklore.net
   Classical fables, mythology and folklore

National Committee for Latin and Greek (NCLG)
www.promotelatin.org
   Resources for educators

Peace Hill Press
18101 The Glebe Lane
Charles City VA 23030
877-322-3445
www.peacehillpress.com
www.welltrainedmind.com
   Susan Wise Bauer and Jessie Wise (*The Well-Trained Mind*)
   Resources for history, science, and language arts

Trivium Pursuit Ministries
Harvey and Laurie Bluedorn
PMB 168, 429 Lake Park Blvd.
Muscatine IA 52761
309-537-3641
www.triviumpursuit.com
   Resources for Christian Classical Education homeschooling.

INDEX

About the Author

Andrew Campbell homeschools his daughter, Julia, works part-time as a freelance copy editor, and helps out with the family business, Tidy Gnome Handcrafts. He holds a doctorate from Washington University, St. Louis, in Germanic Literatures and Languages with a specialization in Medieval Studies. Drew is passionate about education, and has worked as a classroom teacher, a private-school administrator, an independent lecturer and workshop presenter, a private tutor, and a literacy volunteer. He has been researching classical education for over a decade. He and his family live in western Massachusetts.